Unanswerable Questions

Unanswerable Questions:
Ambiguity and Interpersonhood

Andrew P. Porter

WIPF & STOCK · Eugene, Oregon

UNANSWERABLE QUESTIONS
Ambiguity and Interpersonhood

Copyright © 2021 Andrew P. Porter. All rights reserved. Except for brief quotations in critical publications or reviews, no part of this book may be reproduced in any manner without prior written permission from the publisher. Write: Permissions, Wipf and Stock Publishers, 199 W. 8th Ave., Suite 3, Eugene, OR 97401.

Wipf & Stock
An Imprint of Wipf and Stock Publishers
199 W. 8th Ave., Suite 3
Eugene, OR 97401

www.wipfandstock.com

PAPERBACK ISBN: 978-1-6667-1781-5
HARDCOVER ISBN: 978-1-6667-1782-2
EBOOK ISBN: 978-1-6667-1783-9

Manufactured in the U.S.A.

Biblical quotations are from the Jerusalem Bible, c New York: Doubleday, 1966.

Contents

Acknowledgments   vii

Introduction   ix

1   Before the Beginning of the World   1
    1.1   Genesis Rabbah 1
    1.2   In the Beginning 4
    1.3   Ambiguity 6
    1.4   The Inquiry in Prospect 12

2   Persons   13
    2.1   Being Human in Heidegger 15
    2.2   Being Human in the Sociology of Knowledge 23
    2.3   Being Human in Kierkegaard 30
    2.4   Niebuhr on Selves 33
    2.5   The Real Presence of Other People 35
    2.6   Beyond Answerable Questions 37
    2.7   Letter VIII 41
    2.8   Rahner's Supernatural Existential 44
    2.9   Martin Buber 45
    2.10   John Zizioulas 49
    2.11   A Tentative Synthesis 52

3   Language, Self, World, Action   55
    3.1   Getting Into Language 55
    3.2   Language and World 61
    3.3   Language, Narrative, Action 62
    3.4   Language Beyond Propositions 65
    3.5   Unanswerable Questions 67

4	Interpersonation Again	71
	4.1 Beyond All Persons	71
	4.2 Stakes in Life	73
	4.3 Ambiguity Again	75
	4.4 Responsibility	79
5	The Fate of Transcendence	84
	5.1 Irony in Narrative	85
	5.2 Objectivation	90
	5.3 Visible Images	92
	5.4 Proofs	94
	5.5 Analogy	99
	5.6 Acts of God	102
	5.7 Ambiguity and Creaturehood	105
6	Some Sort of Ending	108
	6.1 A Few Answers	108
	6.2 The Work of Christ	110
	6.3 Some Foils	114
	6.4 Kyrie Eleison	115
Bibliography		119
Index		129

Acknowledgments

Some parts of this book are cut and pasted from other pieces of my own writing and without further acknowledgment than this. It is a stage in an inquiry that began years ago in the theology of Edward Hobbs, one that is presupposed on every page. It does not conclude that inquiry. Far from it, it only scratches the surface. So tell your students to do better; this is the best that I can do now. And remember Hobbs's understanding of the beginning of Genesis: we affirm human life in this world as good, in full view of its pains.

Denis Roby was kind enough to read and mark up manuscript printout, with many incisive comments.

I am indebted to Cindy Mason for many conversations. Robert Guyton understands instinctively the ideas in this book and several others before it. I am indebted to Joy and Jed Rowley, who took me to see the play *Assassins* twenty years ago in Albuquerque. George Griener SJ and Mark Fischer helped with Karl Rahner in regard to God's hiddenness and God's self-disclosure. Mark Fischer later was kind enough to comment on the entire manuscript, pointing out many problems in it. Daniel Sportiello apprised me of Curtis Franks' work on rabbinic rules for thinking about transcendence — a salutary caution for all Christian philosophers and theologians. My introduction to Kierkegaard was from my teachers, Robert Goeser and Arnold Come. They opened a new world for me.

My serious introduction to Heidegger was from my doctor-father, Vincent Guagliardo, OP. There are many ironies in my study with a Thomist to learn a little Heidegger, but they need not be recited here.

Over the years I have made a big fuss over the "mistake on page twelve" of *Being and Time*, the mistake wherein Heidegger leaves out other people in the constitution of human being. In hindsight, I have forgotten when I spotted the mistake. It took me years. Few others have seen it; they either accept Heidegger's argument as it stands, or else they get a treatment of other people from other philosophical resources. But it occurs to me that I do remember what was on my mind when the mistake became conspicuous enough to spell it out. It was in conversations and arguments with Alec Blair. His GTU PhD thesis was finished in 1984, arguing that the Old Testament presupposes a corporate structure for human existence, where the New Testament is ambiguous. Many philosophers treat human beings as "generic," that is, as individuals who are all alike and to whom as individuals sociality can be added later. The New Testament can be read either way, but read properly, it builds on the Old and is corporate. So much in brief for Blair's argument. He surveyed many philosophers in his overview of the history, and among them, pegged Heidegger as generic in his anthropology. I defended Heidegger, and Blair never conceded the point to me. My suspicion is that, with a few exceptions, Heidegger's anthropology has to be read as generic (Blair is right). The generic readings are certainly more conspicuous. In any case, it was (I think) in the context of those conversations that the overlooking of the corporate character of Dasein stood out as a mistake — conspicuously so, once it was noticed (more in section 2.1 below). My debts to Alec Blair are enormous.

As said above, Edward Hobbs, my "doctor-uncle," lies behind all of this. He supplied the central necessary presuppositions for the whole inquiry; one of my proofreaders once said to me, "How lucky you were to have Edwards Hobbs as a New Testament teacher!"

Peter Berger himself answered questions, and it was Shaun Sullivan who helped me read through his early and middle work.

This book is probably the culmination of a series, the work of three decades. That work was made possible in a material sense by my Mother's foresight and providence. I don't think it is what she hoped for, except in a very loose way, but her help is here acknowledged.

This book was typeset with LaTeX on Slackware and Debian GNU Linux boxes.

Introduction

This book and its companion, *The Accountant's Tale*, are probably the last in a long series that began thirty years ago. They are an inquiry that I don't expect to finish — too many serious questions remain unanswered. Nevertheless, an interim status can be explained. Long ago as a college student (and like many in today's culture), I was skeptical of Christianity's prospects and would have cited problems with science as the cause. Survey research finds many more like me. Remedies began in Edward Hobbs's New Testament classroom, when he explained that for biblical religion all of life is good, pains included; actions may be evil but being and beings themselves *as* being are all good. The biblical God meets us in all of life, pains included, not just in the fun parts. This is no more than is in Genesis 1–3, but it helps to hear it in different words, as e.g. in Porter and Hobbs (1999). What came to me as an intuitive corollary was that problems with science were dissolved and one could proceed to critical biblical scholarship as the entry into a different way of thinking about Christianity. Over the years and in my experience, the pertinent concepts simply did not work the way most of the culture expects them to work. Unraveling how they *do* work is the larger project of which this book and its companion are only one stage.

The goal of the present inquiry is a phenomenology of *human* action in speaking *of* God and in prayer *to* God. What are we doing with our lives and ultimate reality in biblical religion? How are we related to *divine* action and to divine presence in the human world? Answers will be very incomplete, but such as they are, I hope they can prove a useful beginning for further inquiry.

We explore the implications of two assumptions: (1) that language (our access to the world) is ambiguous, and (2) that in everything humans do, we are always already related to other persons.

These assumptions grew out of earlier work in *The Accountant's Tale*.

They are not complete even in this book, as a little reflection will show.

The themes in *The Accountant's Tale* are three long-running failed engagements in the life of the church. They are (1) objectivation of the faith, rather than responsibility for it, (2) monophysite theology of divine action, or monophysite theology outside of Christology: conceiving divine action as interference with natural processes, and (3) semi-Marcionite theology: beginning Christianity de novo with Jesus and so obscuring the place of Christianity in the history of religions and the foundations of the New Testament in the Common Documents,[1] more specifically in the Exodus.

Objectivation is a way of getting out of responsibility for one's own faith, and in the ancient world, the easiest way to do that was by projecting the faith onto visible images, statues, or idols. There are other ways of objectivating faith, of which so-called "proofs" of the faith are one and alleging objective interference with nature (modern miracles) is another. Aquinas saw both mistakes and avoided them. In his words, "gratia non tollat naturam," grace does not interfere with nature. The Five Ways "prove" only that there is an ultimate reality, not that there is only one and not that it is the biblical God; those require faith. The first two mistakes travel together. The third, beginning Christianity with Jesus of Nazareth, is a little different. It is not in the New Testament, which is based on Exodus typology. Both Christianity and rabbinic Judaism begin with the Exodus, an exodus from nature and nature religion into history and historical religion.

These mistakes have been recognized for centuries, they are recognized in the Bible, but people still clamor for them. Resources are available in biblical, historical, and theological scholarship from the nineteenth century on. One task would seem to be to share this work with the laity, a task for which the clergy have not been particularly eager. The inquiry is the more urgent because the three mistakes above have lost a lot of their credibility for some while others still cling tenaciously to them. Christian theology as the culture imagines it appears to depend on the three mistakes above, and their growing implausibility raises questions about how we really should be doing philosophical theology.

The Accountant's Tale was only the most recent preparation for these questions. *Living in Spin* preceded it by a decade and provided an ontology of human action radically different from what the world assumes by default today. The other books all tried to explain parts of how we relate to a

---

[1] The sacred texts shared by rabbinic Judaism and Christianity.

transcendent ultimate reality, and they were as incomplete as this one will be. Yet hopefully this one will get a little further.

The earlier books left us with questions: How to continue our explanations of Christianity? What are we doing? And in relation to what sort of ultimate reality? Ambiguity of language and neglected interpersonal relations are only two parts of that need to re-understand philosophical theology; others will find more.

In *Spin* and *The Accountant's Tale*, we met Heidegger briefly, as one philosophical development in the last century. Many have noticed that his account of human relations to other people leaves much to be desired, hence this book's interest in interpersonal relations. And twentieth-century work shed a lot of light onto the social and linguistic origins of the world as we know it. Neither of those lacunae could have been filled in the earlier book, which was historical rather than constructive in its logic. That was where *The Accountant's Tale* ended.

How, then, are we to understand our relationship to God? Without conflicts with the natural and social sciences? The sciences grew as a corollary of central idea of creation, the goodness of the world. Part of that goodness of the world is its intelligibility. And should we take into account our own cultural creativity and our own roots in language? These issues have emerged from twentieth-century sociology and linguistics.

It is appropriate to start with language because it is in language that we meet reality. Any phenomenon in the world can be brought to language in many ways, some of which make the phenomenon into something quite different from what we think we understand it to be. Many theories of a phenomenon can touch it, though we would say that some are better than others. But is one the best? Can "the best" of them be found? They are "about" the phenomenon or experience, but what is *aboutness*? Aboutness is human-relative, a feature of the ways in which humans relate to the world. But a phenomenology of relations between humans and the world is barely begun. The Platonist tradition (including Aristotle and Aquinas) seeks explanations that are "the best," independent of whether people know them or not. The approach in this book is different. There are too many possible ways to relate to some phenomenon in the world and they cannot all be canvassed. That ambiguity is a result of prior ambiguity in language. In living with this ambiguity, we turn to our neighbors, other persons. And we still interpersonate even after persons have done all they can. At that point, we are calling on an ultimate reality that we cannot see or grasp.

This is in radical contrast to the Platonist tradition. For that tradition, other persons are the problem; here they are the solution. Hence the alternation of chapters below: ambiguity in language, interpersonhood, more about language, and interpersonhood again, followed by comments on some of the traditional features of transcendence and a few closing remarks.

Chapter 1

Before the Beginning of the World

1.1 Genesis Rabbah

In the Great Rabbinic Commentary on Genesis, it says that six things were created before the creation of the world.

> In the beginning God created:
> Six things preceded the creation of the world;
> some of them were actually created,
> while the creation of the others
> was already contemplated.
> The Torah and the Throne of Glory were created....
> The creation of the patriarchs was contemplated ...
> The creation of Israel was contemplated ...
> The creation of the Temple was contemplated ...
> The name of the Messiah was contemplated ...
> Repentance too,
> as it is written,
> *Before the mountains were brought forth etc.*
> and from that very moment,
> *thou turnest man to contrition, and sayest,*
> *Repent, ye children of men* (Ps. 90.2, 3)

The Great Commentary on Genesis was written some time in the fourth or fifth centuries.[1] Three of the listed things created before the creation of the world presuppose a seventh, language: The Torah, the name of the Messiah, and repentance. The Torah and the name of the Messiah are subtle beyond our present inquiry. It is repentance that is interesting. For repentance presupposes narrative and with it the ability to *re*-tell a narrative, changing one's own acts of willing and if necessary other parts of the story as well. Usually other parts of the story need to be changed, in order to spell out why one now regrets the past. Changing the story does not mean changing the material motions of anything in it (they are physical and cannot be changed, though accounts of them can be corrected). Changing the story means changing what matters, changing what to include and what to leave out. It means choices about how to evaluate the acts told in the story.

What we have stumbled into is the *ambiguity* of narrative, and indeed, of all language. Any story can be told in more ways than just one.

Not only does repentance presuppose language, language presupposes other people, *to* whom the story is told. Other people are easily overlooked.

Ambiguity is the pivot of humor, of jokes: in a joke, we start by thinking we are in one story, and in the whiplash of the punchline we find ourselves in some other story.

I began *The Accountant's Tale* with a joke about a man who wanted to hire someone good with numbers. He interviewed a physicist, a mathematician, and an accountant, and asked each one in turn, "What is 2 times 2?" The physicist's answer was intuitive, the mathematician's was lengthy and complicated, and the accountant replied, "What do you *want* it to be?" *The Accountant's Tale* was a retelling of Christian history from the perspective of the accountant: a history of choices, some open to criticism.

In this book, we are closest to the mathematician, except for one problem: Mathematical questions usually have answers, and when they don't, they can be solved just by fiat. If we don't know how many parallel lines pass through a point not on a given line, we can just arbitrarily decide. That version of the parallel postulate is called Playfair's axiom, equivalent to Euclid's Fifth Postulate. It is pertinent to point out that even in mathematics, the accountant's world intrudes: the parallel postulate is decided by *choice*, not appeal to something demonstrable in mathematics. Outside of mathematics, things are not so simple or so easy, and they may be

---

[1] The quotation is from Midrash Rabbah Genesis, 6. Strack and Stemberger date it between 400 and 450 CE. *Introduction to the Talmud and Midrash*, 304.

more adventurous. In contrast to mathematics, we shall eventually come to questions that do *not* have answers. Our method may seem as arcane as a mathematician's attempt to derive all of mathematics from minimal basics.

We opened with a claim that language was there before the beginning of the world. This is not to claim that language-*speakers* were there before the Big Bang, it is a claim that the structure of the world is, shall we say, *languageable*, already before the beginning, or better, by presupposition. That is a fairly simple claim. The existence of elementary particles (whichever particles you take to be "elementary") may or may not require languageability but the existence of compound structures most certainly does. What holds a composite structure together? That question can be interpreted in at least two ways. In one, the answer is whatever forces hold the thing together, and physics (or chemistry) has those answers. In another sense, "Why are these parts parts of one whole?", to invoke physical forces is to miss the point. Partness and wholeness are not physical concepts, and attempting to capture them within mathematics both concedes that they are linguistic (for mathematics in its own strange way is already language) and also hides their broader meanings. They are a matter of interpretation, i.e. hermeneutics. Interpretation is always already about things that can be languaged.[2] It is in that sense that Genesis Rabbah was right.

It is language that gives human intention the reach it has, far from the physical and temporal present. Only with language can there be a *world*, with all its richness and all the relations of one thing to another. But language is open: anything in the world can be described or intended in more than just one way. And so when we consider some thing in the world, we already have in mind the result of an editing process. We have selected from among things and relations in the world the ones we are interested in.

In its original form, the search for somebody good with numbers was an example of a genre of jokes comparing how different groups or professions interpret a simple sentence. The interested reader may be able to find it on the net.

Though language is ambiguous, this does not reduce it to caprice,

---

[2] To dismiss the question of parts and wholes, and say that material causes are enough, without any *forms*, formal causes, or anything that could do the work of formal causes, is a form of materialism. See my *Living in Spin*, sections 3.3.1 and 3.3.2.

whimsy, or nihilism: We have ways of criticizing claims and narratives. To live in language is to live in that ambiguity. Many things in the world get their being only in language because they depend in their being on other things far from themselves. That is a long story, told in other places. We ourselves are constituted in language, in our relations to other people and to ultimate reality. Very gingerly, we come to the deep ontological questions of the philosophical theologian, thinking like the mathematician in that story. The analog of the physicist is simply assumed: the one who knows the life of faith and prayer on a personal basis, with little theory and less philosophy. One of the fruits of our inquiry will be an obligation to live with uncertainty and ambiguity, and so the philosophical presuppositions of theology will be both like and unlike mathematics. This telling may be different from the usual versions, but all the parts of it can be found in an ordinary seminary education.

1.2   In the Beginning

The Gospel of John begins with a short hymn about "The Word," λόγος in Greek. It is not developed later in that Gospel and it has few ties to literature outside John.[3] Given the ambiguity of language that we already know, let us gloss *logos* as the Joke, to sharpen the challenge of John's prolog.

> In the beginning was the Joke,
> > and the Joke was just The Way Things Are.
> The Joke was *already* there at the beginning.
> Some got it, some didn't.
> Some think the Joke is against them.
> Some trust that the Joke is for us — on us and for us, both.
> Everything that is came to be through the Joke.
> Everything that ever was lived under the Joke.
> All that lives has its life in the Joke.
> In the Joke is life, and in that living Joke is the light of men.
> The Joke shines in the dark,
> > and those who don't get it could not overpower it.

And yes, the Joke comes into the world from time to time. Sometimes one way, sometimes another. (Some say always and everywhere.)

---

[3] Bultmann, *The Gospel of John*, 13–18.

1.2 In the Beginning

> The Joke has been here all along,
> though the world does not recognize it.
>
> The Joke comes to its own,
> and its own don't get it.

Its own are human too.

> In the beginning was the Joke,
> and the Joke was on us.

The Joke was there in the beginning: language (including mathematics) is presupposed from before the Big Bang. Mathematics has at least some of the same sort of ambiguity as can be found in the ambiguity of narrative. As much was discovered in the twentieth century.

Sometimes we get it, sometimes we don't. That, I suppose is a problem, for it means accepting help.

Some think the ambiguity of narrative is against us. Some think it is not the problem but the essential condition for a solution.

A Joke on us and for us, both? That is an act of faith.

> Everything that is came to be through the Joke.
> Everything that ever was lived under the Joke.
> All that lives has its life in the Joke.

In mathematics lie the roots of physics and nature; in ambiguity lies the seed of life as we know it. That's part of creaturehood. Rejecting the conditions of creaturehood is one definition of original sin and that, too, seems to be a part of creaturehood. It's also an example of the ambiguity that comes with language — and the Joke.

> In the Joke is life, and in that living Joke is the light of men.
> The Joke shines in the dark, and those who don't get it
> could not overpower it.

Those who can accept being exposed, who can accept exposure as an offer of grace, should have no problem with this.

> In the beginning was the Joke,
> and the Joke was on us.

For those who are theologically squeamish, remember Job 9.23: God laughs.

In effect, we never know all there is to know about ourselves, about what we are doing, about the world around us. But we can know enough, enough to get through life one day at a time. This underlies all that follows. Language gives us not just ignorance but also ambiguity, and where there is ambiguity, there is choice. Hence the accountant's question, as we saw in *The Accountant's Tale*.

To forget that the Joke is *on* us is to forget the holiness of God. Not to trust that the Joke is also *for* us is to despair of the goodness of God. It is also to miss a central element in the ontological constitution of life, one little noticed and less explored. Life, including language-capable life, depends on that openness and ambiguity. Life (especially language-capable life) is ontologically peculiar in that it construes itself, but that can be done in many ways.

1.3 Ambiguity

This section aims to back up the last two sections, in their claims that with language, many things become ambiguous. We shall merely give examples. A joke requires more than just ambiguity, it needs other people, who can enjoy a joke, and before whom I am exposed in a joke. One thing at a time; begin with ambiguity in language. We will say more about other people in a few pages. In every example that follows, we shall encounter the way that ambiguity is handled: through mattering. Some things matter, some don't. Mattering comes with personhood and it is one of the defining features of personhood but it, too, must wait.

When we come to personhood in the next chapter we shall see life as the sort of being that has a stake in its own being. To have interests is to benefit (or not) from contingency and contingency entails ambiguity. It is what could be otherwise. The future could unfold in many different ways and a living being has to be capable of dealing with them. Life is the sort of being that can cope. To cope is to be able to survive, which is to relate to both self and the world, whether or not a living being knows that. Clearly, life without language does not really know that it is relating to the world, even though we would count some of the more developed animals as very intelligent. Still, without language, they can relate only to the here and now. At the bottom of the scale, a bacterium or a protozoan is only a little more than chemistry. Its relating to the world is something that *we* can remark but a paramoecium cannot. It is language that gives a human

1.3 Ambiguity

animal the *reach* to relate to the distant in space and time. Its capacities for motion give it some *grasp* in the world, but language gives it a reach that extends far beyond its grasp. It is language that enables us to deal with contingency and ambiguity, and that is so whether or not there is anyone actually *speaking* a language. It is in that sense that Genesis Rabbah was right in saying that language preceded the creation of the world. At that stage, language is just possibility, but it is real possibility nonetheless.

To be a living organism, as we know it on this planet, is to be alive in a world, at least in an environment.[4] It would be easy to think that language is just a tool, with which people communicate about things in the world that they already know prior to language.[5] But such a supposition rarely can survive inspection. There may be a few things we know before language but not many. And it is only with the prior possession of language that they can rise to articulation, to *showing themselves* so that we could speak about them. We can speak about things in the world, but they are given to us *as* things in the world only by language. I think it was Peter Berger who someplace said that language, self, and a world are a package, and language is the carrier of the package. We don't *use* language, we *live in* language. It is a given, it is there before us, despite the feature that it can be changed, even by us.

Language gives us ambiguity but it can also resolve ambiguity. It is not as if ambiguity could be canvassed in some phase space that could be mathematized or, pace Augustine, numbered, measured, and weighed.[6] The only thing in common to all the examples of the resolution of ambiguity is *mattering*, mattering to humans, to the sort of being that humans are. The things that matter show themselves. Look at some examples.

Consider first material beings. They are messier than they appear at first sight. They have parts, sub-parts, and raise questions about what *is* a part and what is just something else. It could appear that we are starting with an ontology of solid bodies in transparent media, with ambitions of

---

[4] The difference lies in the possession of language. Language bequeaths a world; without language, animals have only an environment. See the first third of Heidegger, *The Fundamental Concepts of Metaphysics*.

[5] My analysis is somewhat simple, and usually Heideggerian. It relies on others for depth and concrete detail that is hopefully not needed in the present argument. A critique in a Wittgensteinian vein can be found in Ellis, *Language, Thought, and Logic*, especially chapter 2, "Initial Missteps in the Theory of Language."

[6] Many times in *The Literal Meaning of Genesis* (e.g., 6.3.7–8), quoting Wisdom 11.21.

building up everything more complicated from such solid bodies.[7] I think it can be left as an exercise for the reader to show that such a plan already presupposes humans who look at such bodies: that planned ontology is already human-relative. To speak of a material being is to select figure from background. That ability, interestingly, has been very refractory to attempts to duplicate it in artificial intelligence.[8] To distinguish figure from background is to distinguish what matters from what doesn't. It could be called *selection* but that word has some hazards, for it could take us in a mathematical direction that is not as helpful as one might wish. Better words would be to *call* or to *gather* — both of which take us to language, not mathematics, and the reach of language is much broader than that of its restricted version we call mathematics. We gather what *matters*. Mattering is merely presupposed here. It will be implicit in the next chapter, where it is at the core of human being. We shall see it again in section 4.3.

Why is a composite body nevertheless one body instead of just a scattered heap of molecules? It is *mattering* that holds a body together. The idea that chemical bond forces hold it together presupposes that it is all in one piece, but it may not be all in one piece. The combination of a key and a lock will suffice as a counter-example. They are sold together and separated by the user. Neither is what it is without the other, and they are not held together by something naturalistic but by human involvements. Mattering is what explains the choices that call the parts of these bodies to stand out *as* parts of one whole. Mattering is not a naturalistic concept. It appears in no differential equation. It appears in no (natural) scientific theory. It is sometimes presupposed in the way physical problems are constructed, but it is never mentioned beyond the introduction to an arbitrary problem, as in "consider a system of interest." That is a way to hide mattering. Physics tells what happens to some system of interest but "of interest" means mattering. The mattering itself is not part of physics: it is simply assumed, it comes from someplace else.

Move from physics to biology and we see the same thing — and then more. What makes an animal body a coherent whole? Mattering and function. Function is itself an ambiguous concept: both machines and organisms (and their parts) function, but machine function matters to its engineers and users, where organic function matters to the organism itself. Could the parts be arranged differently? Yes, up to a point. Up to what

---

[7] Ellis, *Language, Thought, and Logic*, 15–16, the second misconception of language.

[8] Dreyfus, *What Computers Still Can't Do*, Chapter 6, "Ontological Assumptions."

1.3 Ambiguity

point? Where the changes begin to matter. Could particular molecules be swapped out and replaced by others? Yes. Indeed, any cell could be replaced by another like it.

What about animal body plans? From the perspective of zoology[9] we can begin to see how some animal body plans come in many variations, and that is an intuitive way of dealing only with shapes. Zoology knows many more criteria for the differences between one species and another. Humans can tell, formulas may not be much help, which says that humans can understand the world in ways that theories cannot, or in ways that precede theories.

What about animal *behavior*, to move from material bodies to motions? Aristotle already saw that motions are characteristic of animals in ways that separate them from inanimate bodies and motions (i.e., plants). The future is open, and there are many ways an animal can cope, even at the basic level of finding prey, avoiding predators, and producing offspring. Therein lies the ambiguity of animal motions.

What about shamans and seers, the ancient world's way of handling the ambiguity of the future? A client comes to the seer and asks, "If I do such-and-such, will I succeed? What will happen to me?" Nowadays we don't call them seers, we call them forecasters (weather, the stock market, and so on). Uncertainty has been known from the beginning.

What about narrative, which is how language calls out the motions we know as human actions? A few decades ago, Raymond Queneau, the poet laureate of France, gave us a hundred different ways to tell a simple story:

> One passenger observes,
> as another gets on a bus in Paris,
> with contentious jostling as he does.
> The hat is as odd
> as the head on the neck below it.
> The second gets off,
> and the first later sees him
> in the street near the Gare Saint-Lazare.
> There are remarks about a jacket
> that would fit better with another button.

It is all called *Exercices de Style* and is available to us in a magnificent

---

[9] Thompson, *On Growth and Form*; Raff, *The Shape of Life*.

translation.[10] Are the different tellings all equivalent? Maybe to a logical positivist but not to ordinary people or to poets. What story am I (or are you) a part of? That has more answers than Queneau's tales of a passenger on a bus. Are they all equivalent? Only if you reduce them to propositions.[11]

A classic joke tells the different ways the Army, Marines, Navy, and Air Force interpret the command "secure the building." Told well, the joke can take a long time; there is a lot of military weapons terminology in the responses of the Army and the Marines. It would be easy for a non-military ear to miss the incidental fact that the Army installs guns *in* the building, pointed *out*, to defend it from attackers, while the Marines put their artillery *outside*, pointed *in*, and attack the building from the outside. The Navy sends in three senior chiefs to turn out the lights and lock the doors; the Air Force takes out a three year lease with option to buy. What such a joke illustrates is not just that language is ambiguous, not just that what a sentence means depends on its context, often un-spelled-out background assumptions. It tells us that we often cannot imagine the ambiguities we live in. We are at their mercy.

We all know how to spin a story so that somebody in it comes out looking good — or bad — and other people can do that to me, as well. I can do that to myself, when examining my own memories. I can do that for myself, even when I do not know what I am doing.[12] Humans have a profound and subtle skill of telling what matters — and, at need, of distracting attention from what matters, without ever spelling out what they are doing, even to themselves. Can I summon all the unflattering stories I am a part of, in order to rebut them or neutralize them? No, of course not. That means I do *not* know all the stories I am a part of. Not to know the story one is acting in is surely a form of suffering, whether it feels painful or not. Sometimes we laugh, but with Oedipus in mind, we pray that the unknown stories we are part of will be gentle with us.

Consider the Theban plays as an example of how that ambiguity can wreak havoc and suffering on people. It is not as if we can easily select the ambiguous possibilities that matter and then go on happily with our lives.

---

[10] In English, *Exercises in Style*. The above summary is my own, not Queneau's or the translator's words.

[11] For a long list of ways language tells about the world that go beyond propositions, see Porter, *Basic Concepts of Biblical Religion*, section 5.4, "Living in Language."

[12] Fingarette, *Self Deception*, chapter 3, "To say or not to say."

1.3 Ambiguity

What we don't know can hurt us. The story is familiar enough: in *Oedipus Rex*, Oedipus is predicted to kill his father and marry his mother. Despite reasonable efforts to avoid that fate, it comes to pass. Oedipus makes matters worse with his pride. In *Oedipus at Colonus*, he is old, blind, and a wreck. He carries the burden of his past. His children show up and then dysfunctional family issues are aired. In due course, he retreats offstage and dies. The dialogue surrounding that event emphasizes its holiness: it is sacred ground that may not be trespassed upon. Then in *Antigone*, one of Oedipus's daughters inherits the family mess and finds herself subject to conflicting obligations (ambiguity again), with further tragic results. Their suffering is not entirely their own fault, yet they suffer justly anyway. Life is not fair.

That the bystanders are not allowed to see where Oedipus died and was buried is a way of saying,

> These are unanswerable questions. To try to answer them is worse than just a category error; it is a kind of disrespect that does serious existential harm to all concerned.

As usual, philosophers rush in where even fools have more sense and so we must proceed cautiously. Through the whole sequence, the characters are up against ambiguity and what is unknown but nevertheless very real. They bring tragedy to Oedipus' family. His pride is a form of not respecting that human reality.

Grant that in language we "gather"[13] the things we are interested in, but why do we gather some things and not others? We have seen the answer already: some things matter, others don't. Why do some things matter? Or better, how? And how do we know? That comes in the next chapter. For the present, we simply observe that for humans, things matter. I don't know how to get behind that; for now, it simply has to be accepted.

We shall see more of mattering when we continue the conversation with Heidegger and in more detail there, but we have seen that one thing that underlies his exploration of human being is ambiguity. Without ambiguity, there would be nothing we could call action; not even animal behavior. Is everything ambiguous? No, some ambiguities can be resolved. This, too, requires language. Given the roots of ambiguity in language, we may proceed in chapter 2 to the constitution of persons and personhood.

---

[13] Sheehan, *Making Sense of Heidegger*, 92, quoting from *Pathmarks*.

1.4   The Inquiry in Prospect

The project of chapter 2 is not to prove the "existence" of God; I follow John of Damascus and Thomas Aquinas (among others) in saying that God is not a being that might or might not exist. It does not try to prove that biblical religion (and its God) are the best religion, though I clearly think as much. That cannot be proven because there is no starting point outside of it from which a proof could be attempted.[14] What chapter 2 does is inquire into the structure of personhood in such a way that relating to God could be intelligible — so that relating to God could even make sense. That remains a choice, and clearly many take other choices. Chapter 2 assumes a starting point in Heidegger and foils appropriate to Heidegger. That, too, is a choice, and it may render the book useless for those with no interest in Heidegger, but such people usually have other resources that they like better. Chapter 2 is merely one explanation of what it means to relate to God. There are others.

Chapter 3 will return to structures in language that undergird human social being in the world. Chapter 4 will pull together the previous chapters in such synthesis as is possible thus far. How is it that persons are always already interpersonating toward other persons, both real and possible, intramundane and transcendent? Chapter 5 will bring the previous chapters to some traditional features of transcendence.

Chapter 6 will once again take stock. The inquiry as it stands in the present book is incomplete, as any reader can see. Significant topics in systematic theology are not here. They will require a kind of questioning for which this study may have posed questions, but only that. Answers will await other work, probably by other people.

---

[14] Porter, *Basic Concepts*, sec. 5.6, "Hermeneutical Circularity."

Chapter 2

Persons

We began with barely a manifesto that human life rests in ambiguity, and that ambiguity is inherent in language. Language-capable life has to deal with that ambiguity. From this follow two inquiries, one into personhood and one into the gifts of language. The order is somewhat arbitrary: personhood in this chapter and the functions of language in the next, then returning to personhood again.

What follows in this chapter is a collection of converging arguments or inquiries, all in one way or another supporting the perspective that to be a person is to be related to other persons. After the other persons in the world have done all they can, we still relate as persons. That will take some showing. Among the resources will be Heidegger, the sociology of knowledge, and the ordinary moral capacity for criticizing human actions. But the witness who is both the most strident and the most perplexing would be Søren Kierkegaard, who spelled it out explicitly: to be a person is to be constituted *as* a person by another person (of sorts), a transcendent Other. This, too, will take some work and we must proceed cautiously.

Thus both chapters are collections of several explanations leading together to two theses. Neither chapter is an argument; the merits of biblical faith and the so-called "existence" of God cannot be proven but only assumed, because they are starting points, not conclusions. This has been spelled out in many places in these books. The first thesis is that the personhood of one human being presupposes other persons in communion with the first. The second thesis is that this other-related-ness of human persons extends beyond all particular and generalized intramundane persons. We shall see a hint of that later in this chapter, when we come to Karl Rahner's "supernatural existential," but a parallel development of it will follow from an examination of the place of language in human existence.

The chapter in prospect: Heidegger mostly left out other people, but in some places the omission is conspicuous (sec. 2.1). He gave us a structure of personhood as related to itself and to things in the world. Sociology of knowledge fills in some of the gap in Heidegger: there, other people are of central and original interest (sec. 2.2). Kierkegaard in a somewhat different way shows us how a person relating itself to itself is constituted by other(s) around it (sec. 2.3). H. Richard Niebuhr rebuilt the foundations of ethics (and more, if truth be told) on the presence of and responsibility to other people in everything we turn our attention to (sec. 2.4). We will have then come to the real presence of other people. They are in everything (sec. 2.5). It is possible to ask many questions about life and the world, and all involve other people, but there are some questions that still arise after answers have done all they can (sec. 2.6). Sometimes we proceed alone and feeling alone; other people are present but invisible (sec. 2.7). Karl Rahner saw the primordial human capacity for interrelation as an opening to God (sec. 2.8); it needs to be acknowledged in the present study. Martin Buber and John Zizioulas have seen the problems in Heidegger and offered remedies (sections 2.9 and 2.10). It will then be possible to take stock in a preliminary way (sec. 2.11).

The plan is to present pieces of what will hopefully become a coherent argument: the constitution of human existence in Heidegger, sociology of knowledge, morality, and other sources. These are merely the resources I was aware of; there are doubtless more and perhaps better.[1] They are complementary, and with them all contributing, it will be possible to put them together in an anthropology that tells a little about how persons relate to other persons. It sounds as if persons (i.e., individuals) can be understood before interpersonal relations, but that is not so. Interpersonal relations precede individuals. The illusion that individuals precede interpersonal relations is to some extent foisted upon us by the structure of language. At least that's how it is in English and typical Indo-European languages. Other language families may have better resources.

---

[1] Charles Williams' concept of co-inherence I do not know enough about to include.

2.1 Being Human in Heidegger

We have already bumped into some of Heidegger's arguments, and it is time to spell out what we have stumbled into. We started with language and ambiguity and the interpretive acts of selection ("gathering") by which humans handle ambiguity. The word for gather, λέγειν, has the same root as the word for everything linguistic, λόγος.[2] It is language that enables us to relate to the world and things in it. Language creates ambiguity and sometimes resolves it. We noted in section 1.3 that language allows us to "gather." We asked why we gather some things and not others and we said only that we gather what *matters*. Mattering shows itself along the way in the analysis of human being-in-the-world, a little of which we shall see.

Language is actually not the beginning of Heidegger's analysis in *Being and Time*, and it will help to see how his several interests and contentions all fit together. *Being and Time* is an inquiry into being, as such, and he begins by turning the question around to confront the questioner, the one who asks about being. He begins, under other words, with what we have called "mattering." Human being is the sort of being that can understand being, and (in our words) it can do that because it is the sort of being for whom things and selves *matter*. His words are a little different and they have been translated into English in various ways.

This is not how *Being and Time* begins. As it is commonly read and remembered, he moves quickly from his definition of human being to anxiety as the central feature of human existence, the feature that discloses and makes sense of all the others. Mattering to oneself is what leads to anxiety, and anxiety leads to mortality and thence to temporality. That larger argument we can mostly pass by, not least because it has too many problems and I have neither the ability nor the space here to solve them. One problem that we do address here is the omission of other people in the definition of human being, for correcting that mistake will move the present inquiry toward the recognition of other people in everything, all the way down to personhood itself. Among the other features of his early work, mortality will appear as Limitation below and as the principal challenge to meaning in the cosmos when we come to the sociology of knowledge.

Heidegger calls human being "Dasein," literally "being there," although that is not what he means.[3] In Sheehan's reading (which I ac-

---

[2] Sheehan, *Making Sense of Heidegger*, 92, quoting from *Pathmarks*.
[3] Sheehan, *Making Sense of Heidegger*, 136–137. Even ordinary German does not

cept here) the translation of *Dasein* should never follow its literal meaning. Translators and commentators have proposed many translations and none have made everybody happy. To leave the word Dasein untranslated (as Macquarrie and Robinson do) isn't much better. In English, it is a barbarous neologism, a kind of Heidobabble, jargon. Sometimes we shall just say "human being," and sometimes when a certain kind of clarity or emphasis is needed, we shall follow the example of Macquarrie and Robinson and leave Dasein untranslated.

Look at the definition itself, which is much more interesting. It first appears in *Being and Time* on German page 12. In the Macquarrie and Robinson translation (their p. 32):

> Dasein is an entity which does not just occur among other entities. Rather it is ontically distinguished by the fact that, in its very Being, that Being is an *issue* for it. But in that case, this is a constitutive state of Dasein's Being, and this implies that Dasein, in its Being, has a relationship towards that Being — a relationship which is itself one of Being.

In Joan Stambaugh's translation (her p. 10):

> Da-sein is a being that does not simply occur among other beings. Rather it is ontically distinguished by the fact that in its being this being is concerned *about* its very being. Thus it is constitutive of the being of Da-sein to have, in its very being, a relation of being to this being.

The German (p. 12):

> Das Dasein ist ein Seiendes, das nicht nur unter anderem Seienden vorkommt. Es ist vielmehr dadurch ontisch ausgezeichnet, daß es diesem Seienden in seinem Sein *um* dieses Sein selbst geht. Zu dieser Seinsverfassung des Daseins gehört aber dann, daß es in seinem Sein zu diesem Sein ein Seinsverhältnis hat.

The definition gets repeated here and there.[4]

---

really follow the literal meaning.

[4] Macquarrie and Robinson, 236 / German 191: "Dasein is an entity for which, in its Being, that Being is an issue." P. 182 / German 142, "Dasein is that entity which, as Being-in-the-World, is an issue for itself." Stambaugh, 134 / German 143, "Dasein is a being which, as being-in-the-world, is concerned about itself."

2.1 Being Human in Heidegger

Fortunately, no translator has tried to render the German slang in English slang. The results would have been both appalling and worse than useless. Doing that (as entertainment) is nevertheless instructive, as it illuminates the perils in Heidegger's language. To speak in the slang of the part of America where I grew up, where "at" is not just a preposition but also an adverb,

Dasein itself is where it's at, man!

That does not help, but it tells us something. It resists being subverted by translation into traditional Aristotelian language and then given a place in a neo-Aristotelian technical system. I assume that Heidegger wanted to protect his definition from that kind of subversion. The terms in the English translations (being an issue, being of concern) do not fall into any such (probably Scholastic) trap, and I wonder whether Scholastic philosophy could even express what Heidegger gave us, whether in slang or in the translations.

Here we have several synonyms for mattering: human being is an issue for itself, it is of concern for itself. Later on, Heidegger will focus on *care*: human being cares about itself, whether or not it knows that. There are doubtless more words that could be used as well. There is no way to calculate one synonym of *being an issue* or *care* or *concern* or *mattering* from the others. We are at the mercy of language, and this is an example of why we say we live in language rather than use language as a tool. Heidegger's definition could be paraphrased in English (without the slang) as "human being is the sort of being that is *about* itself," using "about" as a translation of "es geht um." That leaves aboutness unexplained; perhaps it just has to be accepted.

Several observations: Human being bees what it is in a way very different from rocks, tools, rabbits, souvenirs, art, or heirlooms. For the moment, rocks just take up space, they are "vorhanden" in Heidegger's terms. Tools get their being from their usefulness to humans. They are "zuhanden," handy.[5] Heidegger spends a lot of time meditating on tools, for they provide an illustrative contrast with rocks and humans. Animals share some aspects of the being of humans but very little of language. Souvenirs and heirlooms are of more interest to us than to Heidegger.

---

[5] Even beginning students understand this. Hold up a tool of unknown use and ask "What is this? What *is* this?" They know that they do not understand its being until they know what kind of tool it is. One can get out of Heidegger's conclusion about tools only by denying that the language of being means what it says. Yet many do exactly that.

The second point that may be observed in Heidegger's definition focuses on the last phrase in the passage quoted above: A human's relation to itself has the character of *being*, real being, and this is one of the first moves to expand real being beyond merely the being of material objects. What is worth notice is that for Dasein, the being is in the mattering: Mattering is real being. But mattering is invisible, mattering cannot be exhaustively nailed down, mattering is not under conceptual control. Hence materialists don't like it, and they can get away with ignoring it. It is easy for materialists to limit real being to matter and things built up out of matter, not noticing that what holds something built up out of matter together as *one* thing is matter*ing*, which was denied real being. Thus they relegate the being of abstract concepts (including mattering) to some secondary kind of being, perhaps "nominal" being. In Sheehan's reading of Heidegger's project, from beginning to end, there is more to being than just matter, the 'more' comes logically *before* material being and it comes *from* the logically prior existence of something whose only example we know is human being, or human rationality — i.e., language or its logical equivalent. The only being humans can know or deal with is human-relative being. The specification "being, apart from its relationship to humans" is already human-relative, for it already names humans. There is no way to get around that or behind that. One may bracket *some* human-relative features of a thing or phenomenon in the world, but never all of them at once. A commentator on Wittgenstein summarized his position by saying that it is possible to dig up anything — except the ground one is standing on, and the human ability to make sense of the world is that ground.[6]

We are always already present when we consider some thing or feature in the world, and if we are not logically present, there is nothing we can say about it. This is true even of the astrophysical origins of the cosmos, beautiful and indifferent to us as they are. We were not there at the beginning but to even think about cosmogony requires human theories and language. We were not there but languageability was there. If there is other language-capable life, the same applies to them. For astrophysics to be real in any sense that we could imagine requires it to be thinkable and that requires it to be "languageable." This we ventured in the beginning. The fact that the Big Bang occurred 15 billion years before Fred Hoyle

---

[6] Something like that is in Thomas Sheehan's appraisal a recurrent theme in Heidegger. It is impossible to answer why there is a clearing (*aletheia-1*) at all. See *Making Sense of Heidegger*, 73; 75, "... how and why there is openedness at all is unknowable."

2.1 Being Human in Heidegger

sneered at it doesn't matter. Before the Big Bang *was*, Fred Hoyle's (and others') logic *is*.[7]

A third observation may be made, in passing. Human being's structure as mattering to itself and as the one for whom things in the world matter is the basis for understanding the world. Things in the world can matter to human being only because it first matters to itself. The details are somewhat dense and sometimes controversial.[8] They laid the groundwork for much of twentieth-century phenomenology and hermeneutics, but that is a story far from our own.

A fourth observation may be made. It is not particularly controversial. In Heidegger's Daseinanalytik, the human challenge, as the sort of being that understands being, is to understand its own being — instead of fleeing from it or covering it up. The principal feature of human being that matters here is its finitude, or in other words, its mortality. This is not the only way to construe the human problem, as we shall see soon enough.

Heidegger starts with the ontological peculiarity of human beings, but there is more than what he gives us. We have seen the definition above, on his page 12. There is a mistake in it, and it is not in what he says but in what he leaves out.[9] In the original German I don't see how it could even be noticed, but in the translations, once it is noticed, it is a howler. The definition is that human being is the sort of being that has a stake in its own being. So far, so good. But a particular human being is not the *only* human being that has a stake in its own existence. A lot of other people do, too, and it has stakes in their existence reciprocally. Other people had a stake in my being even before I was conceived, never mind born. There are many ways that others can have a stake in my being, or I in theirs, and that opens up a world of possibilities in philosophy that is little noticed and less explored. We shall see some of it, but only some of it. I do not have a comprehensive phenomenology of interpersonhood but that is what we are beginning to investigate.

What Heidegger gives us, in section 26 of *Being and Time*, is often overlooked but it is not negligible. Readers usually view it through the lens of the definition on p. 12, which leaves out other people, as if one could add other people later to individuals already given earlier. Section

---

[7] Before Abraham was, the Joke is.

[8] See Sheehan's comments on the traditional interpretation of the structure of Dasein's being-in-the-world, *Making Sense of Heidegger*, 151–153.

[9] This appeared also in Porter, *Living in Spin*, section 3.4.1.

26 spells out *that* we meet other people in things in the world but it tells less about *how*.[10] How much of "how" can be told is as yet unclear. Some may be presupposed in ways that cannot be gotten "behind."[11] Some surely is open to comment from "in front," in the sense of phenomenology.

Sometimes Heidegger appears to posit individuals before being-with; sometimes he gives us being-with from the beginning. It could appear that he is inconsistent, and it is not always clear whether the text is speaking in his own voice, articulating his own position, or whether it tells the position he is arguing against. Section 26 was only a small part of his argument, and it should have been more than that. He is ambiguous. One can try to shoehorn more than he gives us into what he does give us, but that takes resources beyond Heidegger, as we shall see below. In the end, the reader has to make his own judgements among the possibilities that Heidegger gives us. One possibility is Dasein without primordial involvements of other people, to whom others are added later:

> The expression 'Dasein', however, shows plainly that 'in the first instance' this entity is unrelated to Others, and that of course it can still be 'with' Others afterwards.[12]

This is a relapse into mainstream Western individualism. Unless Heidegger is not speaking in his own voice, or there is more than meets the eye in "in the first instance," it would appear to agree with the omission in the definition on p. 12 and not with the surrounding text in section 26. Yet what follows contradicts an individualistic reading. He seems to understand that being-with is primordial, even if in the present inquiry, we might wish more of some features that he minimizes. He continues:

> ...Dasein in itself is essentially Being-with. The phenomenological assertion that "Dasein is essentially Being-with" has an existential-ontological meaning. It does not seek to establish ontically that factically I am not present-at-hand alone, and that Others of my kind occur.

On an individualistic reading, the presence of others would be merely ontic — and incidental. He denies that. The presence of others is ontological.

---

[10] It says nothing that I could find about how we meet other people (invisible third parties) in the people we meet as "second" parties, face-to-face.

[11] Sheehan in *Making Sense* repeatedly traces phenomena to presuppositions that cannot be gotten "behind," to prior presuppositions; they simply have to be accepted.

[12] Macquarrie and Robinson, 156; German, 120.

2.1 Being Human in Heidegger

> If this were what is meant by the proposition that Dasein's Being-in-the-world is essentially constituted by Being-with, then Being-with would not be an existential attribute which Dasein, of its own accord, has coming to it from its own kind of Being.

He continues in his polemic:

> It would rather be something which turns up in every case by reason of the occurrence of Others. Being-with is an existential characteristic of Dasein even when factically no Other is present-at-hand or perceived.
>
> Even Dasein's Being-alone is Being-with in the world. The Other can *be missing* only *in* and *for* a Being-with.[13]

He emphasizes the point:

> Being-alone is a deficient mode of Being-with; its very possibility is the proof of this.

In other words, being alone presupposes being-with, and so being-with is part of the existential-ontological constitution of human being, as he says in the beginning of the next paragraph. The deficient modes of being-with

> are possible only because Dasein as Being-with lets the Dasein of Others be encountered in its world.

Here he bumps into the personal being of others but declines to investigate.

> Being-with is in every case a characteristic of one's own Dasein; Dasein-with characterizes the Dasein of Others to the extent that it is freed by its world for a Being-with.

In other words, things in the world can be what they are only because the disclosure of their being is shared with other people. As much could be said of other persons in the world, but Heidegger passes over that possibility in silence. What is said of 'Dasein' is true of human being simply but also of any other kind of persons that there may be. Of social but non-linguistic animals, it is true to a lesser extent.

---

[13] Continuing onto Macquarrie and Robinson, 157.

One thing that I can't find even in section 26 is the ontological inter-involvements of one person with others. One person does more than be with other people. Loose and colloquial language would say that we "are a part of" each other, but it is not clear how to develop that. If the translators' language from the definition on p. 12 may be taken as an opening, one person matters to every other, as they do to it, whether or not it knows. It doesn't matter whether he has a theory of interpersonal mattering, and we never know *all* the ways we matter to other people or all the ways they matter to us. Perhaps it would be better to use another word, since "mattering" connotes a conscious acknowledgment of mattering. We have stakes in each other's being, whether we acknowledge that or not.

That is more than what is in Section 26, "being-with." The others are a part of my ontological constitution, even if not literally a part (component) of me myself. It is in this sense that Section 26 offers us only a start at correcting the mistake on p. 12. Once the mistake is seen, it opens up a realm of being that goes far beyond just Section 26.

At least two more features of personhood do not appear in Heidegger. Interpersonal mattering begins before any one individual is born and continues after he dies, so it is in some sense transtemporal. And among the kinds and degrees of interpersonal mattering, some can be made or unmade by personal commitments, as in performative speech acts.

For what it is worth, there seems to be a general consensus that for Heidegger other people are not *wholly* missing, but they were never well explored. Thomas Sheehan:

> (Heidegger is clear that the process of making sense of things is, in the broadest terms, social: "Ex-sistence in itself is essentially being-with." However, it must be said that his take on the social in *Being and Time* is generally negative.) [14]

In summary, we can harvest one thing from correcting the mistake on page 12. Persons are always already involved with other persons; this is part of the ontological constitution of personhood. It is not all of it; persons, as Heidegger saw, are the sort of being that has a stake in its own being, but that always is in relationship to other persons. (We shall see more when we come to Martin Buber's critique of Heidegger in section 2.9.) Human persons at some level know this, whether or not they ever

---

[14] Thomas Sheehan, "What, after all, was Heidegger about?" The quotation is in the 9th page of the online pdf.

read Heidegger. To say this does not yet say much about other persons, particular, generalized, possible, actual, or transcendent. It merely accepts that there are other persons.[15] How the ontological other-relatedness of personhood plays out in the course of a human life is quite variable. Being person-related is an existentiale, underlying all its many possible existentiell expressions.[16]

Where Heidegger doesn't say enough about relationships to other people, sociology of knowledge can offer some help. It is about a great deal more than just knowledge.

2.2 Being Human in the Sociology of Knowledge

Our guide to the sociology of knowledge will be *The Social Construction of Reality*, by Peter Berger and Thomas Luckmann. If other people are rarely thematic for Heidegger outside of *Being and Time* section 26, they are the center and focus of the sociology of knowledge. Heidegger and Berger are complementary. Heidegger gives us resources in ontology but leaves out essential parts. The sociologists supply some of what is missing but at an ontic level and without inquiring into ontology. One difference is that the ontic is merely descriptive, whereas the ontological asks about the logical order of things: Which phenomenon or description is presupposed by the others? What is their logical relationship? All such claims are fragile and probably circular, since they cannot be derived from anything prior. In effect, they are an exercise of human being's ability to understand, to sort out presuppositions. They may be replaced some day by better presuppositions; hence the disclaimer about their fragility. No philosophy is forever beyond comment or improvement — not even Plato and Aristotle.

Heidegger says a lot about understanding things in the world. Interestingly, he says comparatively little about understanding other *people* in the world. It is always about the generic person, of whom you and I and everybody else are instances. With a few exceptions, and apart from *das Man*, Heidegger has little interest in relationships between one person and others, and those relationships rarely have the character of being that is part of the definition of Dasein on p. 12 of *Being and Time*. Colloquially, we

---

[15] This is an instance of the general phenomenon in biology that no species of living organism exists in the singular, but only in the plural.

[16] Macquarrie and Robinson's spelling in translation of *Existenzial* and *existentiell*.

speak easily about understanding another person, but that has not attracted much interest in philosophy.[17]

Sociology of knowledge asks how knowledge is manufactured, distributed, consumed, and used. Knowledge is a social activity from start to finish. Berger and Luckmann someplace concede that their inquiry raises questions for philosophy but they are quite conscientious in never trying to answer such questions themselves. They have bracketed ontology. We, alas, are obliged to speculate, with all the risks that entails. Interpersonhood was mostly omitted in *Being and Time*,[18] and it is here silently presupposed by sociology but without any ontological detail. The ontic expressions that we see in sociality presuppose an ontology that is capable of supporting such expressions, though it does not determine them. We can hopefully recover a little of that ontology from its ontic expressions.

In the perspective of sociology of knowledge, the central problem of human existence is not death but meaninglessness, though they are related. The threat is chaos, a universe whose meaning has failed. It is impossible for the world to make no sense at all; that much we have implicitly from Heidegger.[19] It is nevertheless quite possible for an overarching integrating cosmic reality to crumble and fail.[20] A world is silently assumed, taken for granted, and humans attend to things and tasks in it. But it can fail in at least two ways. In one, its own internal problems may attract attention.[21] In another, as in contact with another culture, it becomes obvious that the cosmos could be understood in some radically different way, and then the cosmos loses its *objectivity* and with its objectivity, its *plausibility*.

Such a cosmos is clearly a human social construction. That becomes obvious when it is possible to see multiple and different socially constructed cosmoi, and one can choose between them. Sometimes one is forced to choose between them. When one is *free* to choose, allowed to choose without loss of approval, then choice is obvious and one is on the

---

[17] Things forbidden in philosophy departments are sometimes investigated in psychology departments under the pretense that they are "scientific."

[18] Heidegger located the daughters of sloth in other people, but we need more than that. For the sources of inauthenticity, see Pieper, *On Hope*, 58. He cites Aquinas.

[19] Meaninglessness is a form of meaning; radical absence of meaning is impossible in Heidegger's perspective on being-in-the-world.

[20] Notice that such meaninglessness is a failure of a previously constructed meaning; it is not how things start, nor could it be.

[21] Berger and Luckmann, *Social Construction*, 165 remark that the disadvantaged are less likely to believe the social fictions than the privileged. When the disadvantaged are successfully stigmatized, there is not much they can do to construct a better reality.

threshold of anomie, lawlessness in the cosmos. With anomie comes anxiety; or better, anomie discloses the anxiety that was there all along, usually covered up, as a part of the human constitution. Peter Berger described cosmogenesis as a human social effort to erect meaning in face of potential meaninglessness. Mortality and meaninglessness are related: Mortality reminds people of potential meaninglessness more than almost any other phenomenon,[22] and meaning is erected in order to domesticate that reminder. They both induce consciousness of an anxiety that Heidegger correctly placed near the ontological center of human being.

Meaning presupposes others with whom it *can* be shared, whether or not it *is* shared. This is not to say that meaning first arises and may then be shared. On the contrary, meaning is always a joint construction, even when the others are present only existentially but not physically and so do not know the meaning that is being constructed. That is one ontological reason why the construction of meaning is always social. We saw hints of it already in Heidegger. (It also presupposes language, to connect with our starting points in this book.) Some of the roots for this were laid in *Being and Time*, section 26.

Berger and Luckmann map three logical stages in which meaning is, in their words, externalized, objectivated, and internalized. Other people are an ontological necessity at every stage. Anxiety or the potential for anxiety is always present also. Look first at these stages of meaning and then consider the anxiety that remains to be reckoned with.

In the end,

> Society is a human product.
> Society is an objective reality.
> Man is a social product.[23]

What starts as something new becomes the structure of society and then must be internalized by those who come later, for whom it already exists outside of their own subjectivity. Why is this? The superficial but nevertheless fundamental reason is that what we see in the creation of institutions applies just as much to all of reality. When legislation creates the institutions by which citizens relate to their government, it starts as something debatable (externalization), but when a proposal becomes law, it is a social institution (objectivation), and those who come later have to

---

[22] Ordinary electric power failures might be a good second.
[23] Berger and Luckmann, *Social Construction of Reality*, 61.

learn how they fit into it (internalization). Countless examples are available from twentieth-century social experience in America, and doubtless in every other society as well.

The ontological roots of this process are easily overlooked in the structure of language. The language by which some meaning is conveyed or some act narrated usually leaves out the other people who are in the background. Yet human acts, meaning, and world are always undertaken with respect to other people, even when they are unknown to other people. In the somewhat strange language of Heidegger's translators, meaning is always "toward" other people. To say that I went to the store to get some sardines is simple enough, and it mentions no other people. But they are present nonetheless, whether mentioned or not. The others are taken for granted, but they are present existentially (and historically) if not physically *before* they could be taken for granted. We share an understanding of sardines, whether we like sardines or not, and any understanding is always toward other people, whether any others are present to mind or not.

Berger and Luckmann do not entirely agree with Heidegger about the theoretical place of what both call the "everyday," or the ordinary world of human activity. For Heidegger, it is tinged with inauthenticity and is a secondary and derivative phenomenon. For Berger and Luckmann, it is where everything begins, and they make no moral evaluation of it. It just is, and it has to be taken for granted. I think Berger and Luckmann's position is the better one. The necessity of accepting the everyday world, even though it could be changed, is paralleled in Thomas Sheehan's exposition of Heidegger.[24] There, the openness of the world to human meaning (Sheehan's $ἀλήθεια$-1) is not something that could *itself* be brought into the light as one more phenomenon among others. It is the presupposition of bringing phenomena into that light, and it accordingly just has to be taken for granted. It is not itself visible; we know it only because we can know that it is presupposed. That is more philosophy than Berger and Luckmann are willing to entertain, but it does parallel their own inquiry.

Externalization is what happens in the process of sharing meaning with others. Berger and Luckmann speak in terms that are philosophically precarious: "The central question for sociological theory can then be put as follows: How is it possible that subjective meanings *become* objective fac-

---

[24] Sheehan, *Making Sense of Heidegger*, 75–76. He emphasizes the disclosedness of the world to humans, which is itself beyond derivation because it is always presupposed.

2.2 Being Human in the Sociology of Knowledge

ticities?"[25] It would be easy to miss the fact that their answers are entirely within the discourse of sociology; "objective" does not mean real (a philosophical question they do not ask), and it says nothing about *how* real things are real. Even within sociology of knowledge, what emerges is quite rich and sometimes surprising. To inquire about how the real is real would take us (for one kind of answers) to Heidegger, or to Thomas Sheehan's commentary in *Making Sense of Heidegger*. There, the real shows itself — but showing is human-relative, part of the *aletheia*-structure of being in the world.

One hazard lies in the appearance that subjective meanings are already possible without the presence of other people. The other people may not yet know, they may not be physically present but they are always already present in the existential structure of the one for whom some new meaning is happening. Yes, a mathematical discoverer may know something new before he tells anyone else but it is important to see that the other people are already present in what a researcher did working alone before he published. Solitary work doesn't make any sense without the existence of other people someplace *for whom* it could eventually make sense. This is to recall the lessons of Section 26 of *Being and Time* and point out that there is more philosophical depth in the social structures Berger and Luckmann depict than they give us — and what they give us is already rich.

In a situation like this one, the customary distinction between the potential and the actual breaks down. The potential is already real and it shapes the actual. This is different from the differences between potential and actual in Aristotle and in mathematical physics.[26] Some possibilities (potential realities) *matter* and others don't. (Once again, mattering shows itself: it is the presupposition necessary to make sense of both human being and of beings in the world.) The possibility of sharing meaning with other people is always already present, and it is what shapes subjective meaning even before that "subjective" meaning becomes real or actual. Indeed, mattering is a kind of meaning, and so mattering itself presupposes the existential presence of other people for whom also it is intelligible.

Berger and Luckmann speak of the "foundations of knowledge in everyday life," but *foundation* is the wrong word. Knowledge is not built on a foundation as a temple is built on a plinth; knowledge is rooted or

---

[25] Berger and Luckmann, *The Social Construction of Reality*, 18.

[26] Neither need detain us. Physics is straightforward; possible being is dealt with under the term "phase space," and mattering is not a category of explanation in physics. Aristotle is best left to specialists.

grounded in everyday life as a tree is rooted in soil. The difference is that in the case of a theory with a foundation, its founding is logically "clear and distinct,"[27] but in the case of reality and everyday life, as with trees, it is impossible to track down all the roots. What is more, some roots could be replaced without loss by other roots.

Berger and Luckmann unfold social structure from three perspectives:

> Externalization and objectivation are moments in a continuing dialectical process. The third moment in this process, which is internalization (by which the objectivated social world is retrojected into consciousness in the course of socialization), will occupy us in considerable detail later on. It is already possible, however, to see the fundamental relationship of these three dialectical moments in social reality. Each of them corresponds to an essential characterization of the social world. *Society is a human product. Society is an objective reality. Man is a social product.* It may also already be evident than [sic; that?] an analysis of the social world that leaves out any one of these three moments will be distortive.[28]

Despite the detail and complexity of the first two moments, in which society is a human product that acquires objectivity, it is the last, internalization, what we are most interested in: Man is a social product. This is easily overlooked in both colloquial and technical philosophical anthropology (though anthropology departments probably do better). Recognizing it is yet one more occasion for anxiety: it means that I am not in control of my own being.

Secondary socialization works only where the novice *identifies* with the novice master. Berger and Luckmann's ontic description here discloses the ontological underpinnings of the phenomenon described. When the new one knows itself as one in whom others have a stake, for whom others care, as one *like* its teachers, then it can learn. Secondary socialization usually enjoys the identification of newcomers with their teachers but that is not always true. It is voluntary. We have all heard horror stories of students trapped in schools that mistreated them. Some students know enough to endure but not to identify with their teachers.

---

[27] Most of the subdisciplines in physics bear such an order relationship to one another, meticulously spelled out.

[28] Berger and Luckmann, *Social Construction of Reality*, 61.

Primary socialization is different: The child has no choice but to identify with the parents, and he necessarily buys into their faults and flaws as well as their virtues, though he has some freedom in how he receives what they give him. The child doesn't know that's what he is doing, though he may learn later, much later. What the child does and becomes make sense only on the assumption that the child and parent have stakes in each other's lives. (In other words, without correcting the mistake on p. 12 of *Being and Time*, nothing can really make sense.) There is no other way, which is why the involvement of others in this self-relationship is ontological. Without it there is at best only an undeveloped human being. At the most basic level, before all theory, learning by identification happens in primary socialization, on which all later secondary socializations are modeled.

All the structures of selfhood are acquired on the basis of their constitution by others. This includes all the structures of the Daseinanalytik in particular. The child can care for itself only because others showed it how, by first caring for it.

All through Berger and Luckmann's treatment of internalization, emotional identification of the child with the parents gets a lot of emphasis. There is more for philosophy here than meets the sociological eye. Emotion is not quite the right term. As far as it goes, it is correct, though there is more. It is a question of whether the young one knows its own being well enough to understand its relationship to its caregivers and teachers. When it does, this understanding is not a *theory* acquired in language, though it is acquired (in important part) in and through language. There is no *theory* in breastfeeding or toilet training, or the "terrible twos"; not for the child and not much for the parents. Theory would get in the way. Yet the child knows, and what it knows is the structure of its own being, even though it does not yet *know* that it knows (or is learning) the structure of its own being.[29] That is what human being is; Heidegger was right: human being is the sort of being that understands (among other things) its own being — including its ontological involvements with other people, to fill in what Heidegger left out. That knowledge is emotionally loaded, and heavily so. So Berger and Luckmann's theoretical reliance on emotion bumps into more than it tells. One place where they spill the beans is when they say

---

[29] The child may *never* learn that his ontology is that of one-who-understands his own being. Fortunately, it is not necessary to read Heidegger to be human. He may be happier not reading Heidegger, happier not knowing how even to spell "ontology."

"we participate in each other's being."[30] As it is, that sentence just adds emphasis within the discourse of sociology; it does not take us into the discourse of ontology. But where Berger and Luckmann do not go, we must.

2.3 Being Human in Kierkegaard

Coming from Heidegger and sociology, we can find a third witness to the structure of personhood that is emerging here. That would be Søren Kierkegaard, from whom we need the definitions in his exposition of selfhood. He can both corroborate our harvest from phenomenology and sociology and also be explained by them. They shed light on each other.

Kierkegaard's project in his writing campaign was a large one, and we need only a small part of it as corroboration of features of human existence that have already appeared in Heidegger and in the sociology of knowledge. His quarrel was with the church of his time and with received ideas about how to believe, how to be human. Along the way, he takes his readers through stages of faith, dealing along the way with Schleiermacher, Hegel, and the earliest beginnings of biblical criticism. Like so many writers in many fields, his central concern is with how to be human, for better or for worse. One may accept one's own selfhood in its givenness or reject it in several varieties of despair. The tension is played out in the phenomenon of anxiety. Heidegger took over some of this, secularized it, and usually removed its explicitly Christian presuppositions.

Kierkegaard in *Sickness Unto Death* spoke of human being as a self that relates itself to itself but is constituted as such by an Other, though that definition gets unfolded in parts, not all in one place. The possibility of despair is part of the original constitution of a human self.[31]

> A human being is spirit. But what is spirit? Spirit is the self. But what is the self?

This merely poses the question; what comes next transforms it.

> The self is a relation that relates itself to itself or is the relation's relating itself to itself in the relation; the self is not the

---
[30] Berger and Luckmann, *The Social Construction of Reality*, 130.
[31] The following quotations are from *Sickness Unto Death*, Hong and Hong trans., 13–14. These are the opening paragraphs of the book, providing the problem of the book and the definitions needed to make sense of it.

2.3 Being Human in Kierkegaard

relation but is the relation's relating itself to itself.

His distinctions in aid of precision are not entirely clear to me. But continue:

> A human being is a synthesis of the infinite and the finite, of the temporal and the eternal, of freedom and necessity, in short a synthesis.

These dimensions of synthesis will occupy Kierkegaard at length. He continues, after some qualifications:

> If, however, the relation relates itself to itself, this relation is the positive third, and this is the self.

Now comes the crux:

> Such a relation that relates itself to itself, a self, must either have established itself or have been established by another.

He continues momentarily:

> The human self is such a derived, established relation, a relation that relates itself to itself and in relating itself to itself relates itself to another.

At this point, there is no justification for the last clause ("and in relating itself to itself relates itself to another"). The structure of relating to oneself is already, in and of itself, a way of relating oneself to other(s). This is not intuitively obvious. It would be so much easier to separate relating to oneself and relating to others.

Next comes the first hint of a major theme in the work:

> This is why there can be two forms of despair...

The two despairs are well-known: the despair of giving up, of not even trying to be the person one has been given to be, and the despair of defiance, trying to take over for one's self the making of one's self. Two things are asserted here, more or less explicitly: To be a self is a task, something (apparently[32]) to be accomplished, and to be a self is to be related in a

---

[32] I say *apparently* to be accomplished because it does appear that way in casual readings of Kierkegaard, though Kierkegaard explicitly rejects that reading.

personal way to some other — whom is not yet specified. Selfhood as a task is taken over in Heidegger, in the distinction between authenticity and inauthenticity. Other people Heidegger mostly overlooked, as we have seen.

Better than asking what does a self have to *do* to be a self would be to ask, "What has to *happen* for a self to be in right relationship to itself and to the other(s) that constituted it as a self?" In traditional language, that leaves room for grace, which the self may accept or decline. Kierkegaard does not use traditional language. He poses the further problem thus. One who sees his own despair (of defiance)

> ... with all his power seeks to break the despair by himself and by himself alone — he is still in despair and with all his presumed effort only works himself all the deeper into deeper despair.

In a right relationship,

> The formula that describes the state of the self when despair is completely rooted out is this: in relating itself to itself and in willing to be itself, the self rests transparently in the power that established it.

The Other Kierkegaard was interested in was, of course, God. The self that relates itself to itself reappeared in Heidegger as the sort of being that has a stake in its own being, is concerned about its own being, etc. God does not play the role in *Being and Time* that he did in *Sickness Unto Death*.

For Kierkegaard, the self is directly in relationship to the Other that constituted it as a self. That is to move a little faster than we should in a careful phenomenology. With the results of our visit to sociology of knowledge, we are in a position to say that Kierkegaard's self is (in time) first constituted by others, many others, before we can entertain his questions about a transcendent Other. Both approaches, one starting from ordinary others, one starting from a transcendent Other, are needed, and we need to see how to get from others to the Other. Inasmuch as the first is intramundane and the second is about transcendence, the character of the logic will change along the way.

2.4 Niebuhr on Selves

H. Richard Niebuhr's thinking on selves and selfhood appeared in several places, all written at about the same time but not all published together. It was not a central issue in *Radical Monotheism* (first published in 1960, with supplementary essays in 1970). It was central in *The Responsible Self* (1963) and central again in *Faith on Earth* (published in 1989 but written about the same time as *Radical Monotheism*). The issue in *The Responsible Self* was responsible action in ethics and narrative; in *Faith on Earth*, it was interpersonal trust and betrayal.

Niebuhr wanted to make sense of ethics in terms of responsibility, an acting person's relations to other people.[33] In so doing, he sought resources beyond the principal strands in the tradition, of which Aristotle and Kant are the exemplars. His summaries of them are cursory and just enough to get on with what he was really interested in. The principal source was George Herbert Mead (among a few others),[34] but as usual, when Niebuhr built on other sources, he made them his own — rebuilt them, in effect.

In seeking a basis for ethics in man the responsible actor rather than man the good-seeker or man the law-keeper, Niebuhr explicates action in terms of narrative, though he does not use that word.[35] Action begins with a question, "What is happening here?" That presupposes a narrative. An actor responds to others' prior actions and anticipates their further responses. He does so in a community of narrative-competents, persons who can criticize the narrative he assumes and criticize his actions in it. That entails that for his actions to have *meaning*, they have to be intelligible to others. That is part of the constitution of meaning, or perhaps we could say that other persons are part of the ontological constitution of meaning.

The relationship of interpersonal meaning scales both up and down. The human self is built on it:

> To be a self in the presence of other selves is not a derivative experience but primordial. To be able to say that I am I is not an inference from the statement that I think thoughts nor from the statement that I have a law-acknowledging conscience. It is, rather, the acknowledgment of my existence as the coun-

---

[33] H. Richard Niebuhr, *The Responsible Self*.
[34] Mead, *Mind, Self and Society*.
[35] Niebuhr, *The Responsible Self*, 61–65.

terpart of another self.[36]

He continues a few sentences later, that a human being "knows itself in relation to other selves but exists as self only in that relationship." George Herbert Mead observed that the human self is an object for itself. This is not exactly what Heidegger said about human being, but it is the same phenomenon, the same relationship of a human self to itself under another description.

> [H]ow is it possible that a being can become an object to itself? Only, Mead argues, through dialogue with others. To be a being that is an object to itself is possible genetically and actually only as I take toward myself the attitude of other selves, see myself as seen, hear myself as heard, speak to myself as spoken to.[37]

Niebuhr surveys the social theory available to him and then generalizes that anything of interest (or any person, not just things) occurs in a triple context of self, others, and thing (or person) of interest. Something or someone of interest always occurs in a context with a knowing subject and a community of other knowers. In most of the tradition, I think the relation of knowing has been construed as two-sided: just the knower and the known, prescinding from any other knowers. Niebuhr calls it a "triadic" relationship, one that includes the community of those who can criticize knowledge, a community that may not be bracketed because it is an essential part of knowing anything. It isn't that we know together as a community, thus abolishing individual persons or rendering them some kind of epiphenomenon. Rather, individuals can know only in a community that can criticize their knowing. That does not mean the community is sovereign; it may indeed be wrong, as prophets and dissenters have labored to point out, sometimes succeeding in persuading their communities. Disagreement (like agreement and corroboration in community) presupposes the presence of the community. Without it, there is merely a kind of isolated individual that only a philosopher could imagine.

Niebuhr's inquiry in *The Responsible Self* was intended as a basis for ethics, and it is worth spelling out a little of that, sometimes beyond what Niebuhr himself said. With resources in sociology and Kierkegaard already in hand, it is possible to see a little more of that basis for ethics.

---

[36] Niebuhr, *The Responsible Self*, 71.
[37] Niebuhr, *The Responsible Self*, 72.

As Niebuhr has it, to be human and capable of human action is to be in response to other humans. As Berger and Luckmann observed, in primary socialization we both receive and learn a world, roles, rights, and responsibilities. We internalize a *social* world. This means that when we act, when we do anything at all, we are always doing something others approve or disapprove of. In effect, moral criticizability is built into human action. The criticizability of human actions simply has to be accepted; particular criticisms do not. This says nothing (so far) about making sense of actions or what sorts of actions should be approved or disapproved of. That comes later, logically. For the moment it is important to observe that it is possible to be disappointed in actions, both one's own and others. Taking offense at acts is another aspect of disappointment. They are not quite the same thing as liking or disliking another's actions. The original word in the New Testament, taken from surrounding culture, was ἁμαρτάνειν, to miss the mark. It was restricted to mean *sin* in the Christian literature that followed, and it (and its relatives) had already occurred many times in the Septuagint.

As we have seen already, the human problem for Heidegger was anxiety and mortality. For the sociology of knowledge, it is cosmic meaninglessness. Once the moral character of human being is seen, it is disappointing human action, focused in the concept of sin. Thus it was with St. Paul, especially in Romans. Niebuhr in *Faith on Earth* took issues of trust and betrayal as an opening to acts of God.

2.5 The Real Presence of Other People

At this point, we are in a position to collect a result worth a little emphasis. Correcting Heidegger's mistake in the definition of human being, we saw other-people-ness in everything and everyone. It appears in various ways, some seen, some not; some voluntary, some not; some more important than others. Call it the real presence of other people.

Heidegger himself occasionally bumped into it, spelled out a little of it, and then returned to his chosen path through the Daseinanalytik.

> In our 'description' of that environment which is closest to us — the work-world of craftsmen, for example, — the outcome was that along with the equipment to be found when one is at work, those Others for whom the 'work' is destined are

'encountered too'.[38]

The further exposition in section 26 shows us other people, with whom we live, and who are beings like me or us, whoever the me or us happens to be, but it never explores the mutual stakes and involvements we have in each other. For Heidegger I am always *with* others, but I am not *part* of the other's being (nor are they part of mine). We disagree. I would say the existential presence of other people is a necessary part of the constitution of any person. This is more than simply being with other people.

For the present inquiry, other people are part of the ontological constitution of everything and everybody, even though they are not part of — not components of — other things and people. This is enough to make them present in everything and everybody, hence the "real presence" of other people. If real being consists in the mattering of things, in the disclosure of things in ἀλήθεια-2 (Sheehan,[39] grounded in ἀλήθεια-1), then that mattering is always mattering for many people, not just individuals, even though we tend to focus on individuals. Being-in-the-world is always shared, even when people disagree about the world and things and people in it. Ἀλήθεια-1 is interpersonal, not as a contingent fact but in principle. The disclosure of the world is interpersonal as a part of its ontological structure, as part of how it exists, not as something that is added on to a prior disclosedness to individuals.

As a corollary, it is possible to comment on one of the definitions of truth that has run through the history of Western philosophy, the notion that truth is the correspondence of a judgement with things in the world, *adaequatio intellectus et rei* (sometimes *ad rem*), etc.

> The translation of ἀλήθεια as "truth" should be strictly and exclusively confined to this third level: apophantic correctness. This is the locus of the traditional (Aristotelian, Thomistic, Kantian) doctrine of truth as the conformity of the judgment and the judged, the agreement of mental or verbal propositions and worldly states of affairs.[40]

The problem with any such definition of truth as correspondence is that both what gets blithely called "judgement" and what gets called "res, rei,

---

[38] Section 26: Macquarrie and Robinson, 153; German, 117. It should be clear that Heidegger's position here is not pan-psychism, nor is my own. We meet other users *with* the tool but not *within* the tool.

[39] Sheehan, *Making Sense of Heidegger*, 73.

[40] Sheehan, *Making Sense of Heidegger*, 77.

rem" are many-featured phenomena. Judgement in particular is a radial category (as George Lakoff would have it), rather than something as simple as a Cartesian would make it. This is incidentally why the issue has evoked so much philosophical comment from the beginning to the present. In a radial category, the different meanings of a word or concept are all analogically related to one another, and possibly to a hub or prototypical meaning, but the analogies are not calculable. They simply have to be learned[41] and can only be learned by one who is actually human by virtue of having stakes in the world and fellow humans. The reason is that analogies are all human-related; two things are analogous *for humans* (and in a particular culture). Analogy is not something from which human involvement can be abstracted. Hence in any successful adaequatio there are other people, and this is a particular instance of the general presence of other people. In other words, truth (in this case, *adaequatio*) rests on *troth*.[42] How that is can be simple or subtle. When I trust a proposition, I am trusting the other people, known or unknown, who have proposed it to me, who share a world with me. Obviously that trust is fallible — on both sides.

2.6 Beyond Answerable Questions

The logic of the inquiry here has a model. We ask about human interpersonhood, the constitution of personal being as always already related to other persons, as always *ready* to relate to other persons. Then we ask, what about when available other persons have done all they can? What about when they don't satisfy the need as it is experienced? The model for our answer to questions about *persons* is a prior inquiry into questions asking *why*. It was explored by D. Z. Phillips in *The Problem of Evil and the Problem of God*.[43] There Phillips marked a deep divide in basic presuppositions in philosophy of religion: Some misunderstand why-questions when they are directed at transcendence (i.e., at God). They think these why-questions can be answered in the same way ordinary intramundane why-questions are answered. Phillips points out that when people ask such why-questions it is *after* answers have done all they can. They still ask. It is fair to observe that the logic of questioning has changed at this point.

---

[41] Lakoff, *Women, Fire, and Dangerous Things*, chapter 6, "Radial Categories."
[42] See also Porter, *Basic Concepts*, sec. 5.5 and *Living in Spin*, sec. 8.3.
[43] Phillips, 133–134, quoted in Porter *Basic Concepts*, 82.

I propose that something similar is going on when we relate — and pray — to God. Other persons have done all they can; we still relate as persons, but to whom, if there is no person there to relate to?

It would be tempting to take God as the asymptote to which intramundane persons approach in some ideal limit. That won't work, because it would put God within the world just as we put real numbers on the same line as rationals, subject to the same laws.[44]

One reason we look beyond intramundane other people is that they are often wrong or just can't help. Even when they are right, as far as we can see, they are still culturally conditioned, and we don't have the power to survey reality from any standpoint that is *not* culturally conditioned. So what is it, in logic, that takes us beyond them? What could it even mean, to say that they are wrong? Wrong by what standard? In comparison to whom? If they are wrong, who is right? Is it possible for everybody to be wrong and need some other source of right? It has certainly happened; just look at the history of science, at any time when a paradigm accepted by all was replaced by another that was quite different. We are not troubled when new research shows that everybody was mistaken about something; in fact, we rejoice.

Together, we face the problems of meaning, mortality, and morals, and together we need a transcendent Other. The Other cannot be logically on all fours with other humans, though it is to be met on a personal level. One can declare this relating personally after all other persons to be a category error, and ban the practice of prayer, but that is not an argument, it is a demand. It was the move of logical positivists in the twentieth century. Whatever the positivists said, they treated the interpersonal relating that engages transcendence as of the same kind as the interpersonal relating of ordinary human social contexts. If we decline that assumption, then what? The logic of transcendence and of human relating to it now becomes somewhat odd. Some of that can be seen in Phillips' book, *The Concept of Prayer*, in which he showed that the logic and semantics of prayer are indeed quite peculiar, even though the syntax of the language of prayer is for the most part the same as that of ordinary conversation.

When we relate to God, we are not relating to another person, one being among other beings. This much is not new, though it is largely

---

[44] See for example, Hamilton, *Numbers, Sets, and Axioms*. The work was done in the nineteenth century by Cauchy and Weierstrass. For those without mathematical experience, it simply has to be accepted that the limit of a series of items within the world is still another item within the world, even if it is not another item in the original series.

forgotten. Aquinas said that God is not a being among other beings when he effectively said that God does not exist in any meaning of 'exist' that we could understand.[45] To be tedious, there is a God, and he does many things, but existing is not one of them.[46] It is possible to obfuscate the matter because it is so easy to equivocate on the meanings of 'to be,' *esse*, 'exist,' and so on. Only beings can exist, and God is not a being. If God existed, he would not be God, he would be a creature. Why do beings exist? Why is the world intelligible? These are unanswerable questions. Scholastics speak of "the act" of being, by which they mean in some sense that the being of beings is the result or consequence of acts of God. In simpler language, the answer to "Why do things exist?" is "They just do." One-syllable words. In the language of insurance brokers, it is an act of God, and insurance brokers would probably be embarrassed (or insulted) to be mistaken for philosophers, but their language is nevertheless more perceptive than they are willing to admit.

One could forbid all talk about unanswerable questions but that, again, is the move of logical positivism and its friends. Why the prohibition? Because unanswerable questions make positivists anxious and that, too, tells more than it appears to. (The fact that a question is unanswerable does not always mean that it is uninteresting or meaningless.) Anxiety comes when we overhear someone we know well talking to someone else who is not there. We are used to bag ladies talking to someone who is not there, but when a friend who is respectable and able to cope in society does it, it can be profoundly unnerving. The anxiety goes away (with great relief) when, moving slightly, we can now see a telephone cradled on the talker's shoulder. He *is* talking to a real person, he is not crazy. As said, we are used to this with a bag lady on the street talking to someone who is not there, but the challenge is tamed because we know bag ladies do that, and we have the social skill of ignoring them. They make existential demands on us, but we know how to fend off such demands. They are not a threat to the stability of the cosmos or the meaning of life. We know also (if we have any experience with liturgy) that common prayer can be dismissed in a similar way. It, too, can be defanged. It is too easily domesticated.

---

[45] In the commentary on the Sentences, *Super Sententiarum* 1.8.1.1 ad 4. It is quoted in my *Basic Concepts*, among many other places. See Murray, *The Problem of God*, 72; Rocca, "Aquinas on God-Talk," 648–649; Rocca, *Speaking*, 65. This text is early in Thomas's career, but the *Summa* is late, and ST 1.13.13 ad 1 says we can know basically nothing about *what* God is, and that is close to the same thing.

[46] See also pp. 95 and 96, when we come to John of Damascus below.

Maybe that is necessary; maybe not.

It would appear that the term 'God' is one place in language where we engage unanswerable questions. The syntax appears to answer those questions (it takes the form "God did such-and-such," in the usual intramundane way) but that is not what is meant or understood. If the syntax and the semantics are contradictory, too bad, and too bad for the irony-challenged.[47] Stephen Mulhall observed that for analytic philosophy, an apparent contradiction signals a dead end, but for Continental philosophy, a contradiction may be a window into what is quintessentially human — the way into something really interesting.[48] In a sense, when we relate to a transcendent Other, we are relating at a personal level to what is not "a person." One possibility is that that is just a category error (cf. Mulhall's contradictions) and should be dismissed accordingly. Another possibility is that we know we are committing a category error, and do so in order to say things that can be said in no other way — both *to* God and *about* God. Prayer is not for the irony-challenged. Indeed, one could say that most talk about God is based on deliberate category errors. When that is obvious, the ironies may be heard. When it is forgotten, trouble is not far behind, as the history of post-medieval theology and its outcome in the modern world well attests.

If "God did it" is taken in multiple senses by different believers, ranging from monophysites of divine action (Humean miracles, creationists) all the way to John of Damascus or beyond, that just means the language is ambiguous. This book began with ambiguity; we don't have much control over it. The Church has known about some of that ambiguity from the beginning, as in the pejorative remarks in the Gospels about signs and wonders, which they nevertheless tolerate.[49] In effect, many treat language of divine action as if it were *not* a category error. The Church has tolerated such language to the point of indulging it, often protecting the naive from the not-so-naive who might challenge them to grow in their faith. We shall return to these questions in sec. 3.5, "Unanswerable Questions."

---

[47] Could we devise language with a syntax that better reflects the semantics of transcendence? I do not know.

[48] Mulhall, *Philosophical Myths of the Fall*, 12–13.

[49] See also *The Accountant's Tale*, chapter 8, where the issues surrounding signs and wonders get more discussion.

2.7 Letter VIII

It could seem that God has made us for himself but then skipped town — absconded, left us alone, abandoned. That appearance is incoherent, for if God has made us, then he is present here with us, whether or not we can see him. That much is implicit in construing the being of human beings as the result of an *act*, and we have seen this already. Sharpen the quandary by stating it more carefully: Persons have in their structure and ontological constitution a readiness for involvement with other persons, a being-toward-person(s). Without some exercise of that existential faculty, a human has not really become a self. If one accepts the appraisal of this book,[50] people seek something personal even after other persons in the world have done all they can. Hence the turn to transcendence.

Our predicament could be redescribed by saying we see no traces of any such Other Person. Yet even this is not as coherent as it appears to be. We are using language with a semantics beyond its normal usage. For a Person within the world would not be transcendent. To seek such would be like looking for $\sqrt{-1}$ on the real axis; it isn't there, and the quest is incoherent. Many people have devised events in the world onto which they can project their sense of awe and wonder, events that seem to represent the inbreaking of divine action in a way that works the same way as ordinary intramundane causation. Such claimed events are "objective." They take the responsibility of faith on themselves, absolving the believer of responsibility. The Gospels call this belief in "signs and wonders," and though they tolerate it, they don't like it, and all four say so explicitly.[51]

So in seeking a transcendent Other beyond anyone who could "exist," an almighty Nothing to whom we can relate personally, we inevitably find ourselves in a certain kind of desolation. C. S. Lewis meditated on this feature of life and faith in *Screwtape*, Letter VIII. The ending of Letter VIII is very memorable:

> Do not be deceived, Wormwood. Our cause is never more in danger than when a human, no longer desiring, but still intending, to do our enemy's [God's] will, looks round upon a universe from which every trace of him seems to have vanished, and asks why he has been forsaken, and still obeys.

---

[50] Not just this book; see also Porter, *Basic Concepts*, chapter 6.
[51] See Matt 24.24, Mark 13.22, John 4.48; and Luke 11.29.

The preparation for that punch line is less memorable and more painful to assimilate. Wormwood has noticed that his patient goes through cycles of comfort and something that is a combination of loneliness, abandonment, boredom, desolation and the like. There are no traces of God at the moment. Wormwood is hoping to exploit these dry periods, as something like an opening into which to drive a wedge between his patient and God. As Screwtape explains, Wormwood misunderstands totally. These "dry" periods are not just part of the cyclical character of human existence as a synthesis of the animal and the spiritual, body and soul. 'Synthesis' should have invited liaisons with Kierkegaard, among others, but Lewis did not pursue that opening.

Has no one ever told you about the Law of Undulation?

Cycles in what Heidegger would call attunement to the world (and to God) come and go, and they are rooted in human nature.

> Humans are amphibians — half spirit and half animal. (The Enemy's determination to produce such a revolting hybrid was one of the things that determined Our Father to withdraw his support from Him.)

He continues:

> As spirits they belong to the eternal world, but as animals they inhabit time.

I would say Lewis is being generous to animals; they don't understand time the way we do. What he calls "the eternal world" could well start with a Heideggerian observation that the 'mattering' in Dasein's mattering to itself and others has the character of being, real being. That is a doorway into a world beyond the naturalistic world of matter. It is incidentally transtemporal.

We come to the crux:

> Now it may surprise you to learn that in His efforts to get permanent possession of a soul, He relies on the troughs even more than on the peaks; some of His special favourites have gone through longer and deeper troughs than anyone else.

After a little about the different reasons and aims of God and the devil, Lewis continues:

> You must have often wondered why the Enemy does not make more use of His power to be sensibly present to human souls in any degree He chooses and at any moment.

In words from the Gospels, signs and wonders; in a word from the modern world, the world of Hume and after, "miracles." Lewis, like the Gospels, allows belief in "miracles," avoiding the modern and postmodern questions about whether they "really happened." People use "miracles" to objectivate their faith, to get them out of responsibility for their own faith, to conceal the human origins of religion as a human social construction. Lewis dodges all that.

> But you now see that the Irresistible and the Indisputable are the two weapons which the very nature of His scheme forbids Him to use.

Lewis doesn't much like signs and wonders, though he tolerates them. Growth in faith means getting along without "visible" signs of God and learning to see the presence of God where it shows itself without the "indisputable."

In Lewis's view, the troughs are, in a sense, sent by God. God is indeed present when the patient feels his presence in warmth and comfort — and without anxiety. Nevertheless, God values the patient's spiritual progress most when the patient cannot see Him, when God seems most absent, when the world seems most God-forsaken. For it is then that we come up against the invisible presence of other persons in everything we deal with, and so also, with the personal beyond all persons.

This chapter has been about other people, and they appear to be missing in Letter VIII, but the other people whom Lewis left out in Letter VIII he supplies in Letter IX. There, Screwtape instructs Wormwood never to let his patient find out that other people have been through the desolation he is going through. Never let him find out that he is not alone: "You have only got to keep him out of the way of experienced Christians." What concrete and particular other people make clear is that when we meet someone or something in the world, we always do so in company with other people,[52] and that is true also when we respond personally to a reality that is beyond all persons.

---

[52] As we saw in section 2.4, on H. Richard Niebuhr's reading of George Herbert Mead.

2.8   Rahner's Supernatural Existential

Karl Rahner spoke of what he called a "supernatural existential," meaning an inbuilt openness to God in all human beings. One may rightly ask whether the supernatural existential is the same thing as what one gets by seeing and correcting the mistake on page 12 of *Being and Time*. I would say they are *about* the same thing but not exactly in the same way. Heidegger didn't do much to help us fill in the omission on page 12, and Rahner's treatment of the phenomenon is at bottom Scholastic rather than Heideggerian, despite the use of a few Heideggerian terms in an otherwise Scholastic context. Rahner doesn't fill in in Heideggerian terms what Heidegger left out. His problematic was Scholastic, and that was probably a constraint imposed by his context — his conversation partners (Garrigou-Lagrange, de Lubac, and others) were already in a conflict between the older Scholasticism and la Nouvelle Théologie. To have explored what Heidegger left out in Heidegger's own terms would have produced only bewilderment.

One helpful guide can be found in a 2004 article by David Coffey.[53] He traces the supernatural existential from early to late in Rahner's published work. Rahner's own comments begin with a German article in 1950, responding to earlier papers by others.[54] Rahner's first German version[55] appeared only a little changed in Cornelius Ernst's translation, "Concerning the Relationship between Nature and Grace," *Theological Investigations* 1 (1961) 297–317. The ideas were restated in several places, the latest of which was in *Foundations* (1976).[56] In the end, the treatment is still in latter-day Scholastic terms, and the question of how to interpret (and correct) Heidegger was not raised. Coffey (109–110 and 116–117) appraises the work as at bottom Scholastic, and on his p. 117 says he has constructed a Scholastic account in order to be more reader-friendly to his likely Catholic audience. While one can certainly use the Scholastic ideas as a guide in exploring what Heidegger left out, a Scholastic inquiry is better left to specialists. In effect, Rahner has filled in — in Scholastic terms and for Scholastic purposes — what was missing in Heidegger's own ac-

---

[53] Coffey, "The Whole Rahner on the Supernatural Existential." *Theological Studies* 65 (2004) 95–118.

[54] See Coffey, his footnote n. 1.

[55] Rahner, "Eine Antwort," *Orientierung* 14 (1950) 141–145.

[56] Karl Rahner, *Foundations of Christian Faith*, section IV.3, "The Offer of Self-Communication as 'Supernatural Existential'."

count, without trying to debug the text in *Being in Time*.[57]

It is fair to note in passing that the Scholastic problematic is quite different from Heidegger's: it is about nature and grace. Grace does not appear in the Daseinanalytik, and though nature is common enough, it does not appear in contrast to grace. Heidegger was not interested in the problem of nature and grace.

Some of Rahner's remarks may help to pull together the threads of this chapter. Rahner apparently once said that after all the pain and suffering of this life, much of it inexplicable, God doesn't give reasons for what happens to us and he doesn't justify himself to us. It may not even make sense to think he *has* reasons that he doesn't give us. What he gives us is himself, not reasons.[58] To say that is to approach the problem of this chapter from the other side. What the chapter argues (as Rahner did) is that we are always able to receive that gift.

2.9 Martin Buber

Where Rahner did not try to find the problems in *Being and Time*, Martin Buber did, and he leaves us a fairly incisive diagnosis in his comparison of Heidegger and Kierkegaard.[59] While Buber did not spot the critical mistake on page 12 of *Being and Time*, he did lay out many of the consequences of the mistake, especially as they stand out in comparison with Kierkegaard. Kierkegaard's man is anxious in face of God; Heidegger's is anxious in face of himself — which is not the same thing. Heidegger has secularized Kierkegaard on the way to his own anthropology, and a great deal has been lost.

It is my claim that anxiety in face of oneself presupposes interpersonation, even when there are no other intramundane persons to relate to personally. Anxiety in face of oneself is an *example* of interpersonation when there are no other intramundane persons as focus of that anxiety. (Usually there are *also* intramundane persons, at least virtual persons or possible persons, who can stand in before one runs out of intramundane others and still interpersonates.)

The challenge, then, for a philosophical theologian is to speak of God

---

[57] As noted above, the original German is not very helpful, and Rahner presumably did not work from the English translations.

[58] The source and text are in in Porter, *Basic Concepts of Biblical Religion*, 88–89.

[59] Buber, *Between Man and Man*, part V, "What is Man," 157–180.

as the pertinent Other without turning God into yet another person among other persons — one being among others, possibly omnipotent, omniscient, etc. I side with those for whom God is not a being among other beings. It may be that we get no further than pointing out that we relate personally to a reality that is not a person, leaving it to others to reason beyond that threshold if such reasoning is even possible.[60] Nevertheless I think many questions about what we are doing have not been noticed, much less answered. Let us first hear a little more of Buber's criticism of what is left out in Heidegger.

Buber's contrasts between Kierkegaard and Heidegger begin with guilt, *schuld*, in Heidegger.[61] It is not the same as in Kierkegaard. "The call of conscience sounds into this situation. Who calls? Existence itself. 'In conscience the existence calls itself.'" Buber continues, giving us Heidegger's position: "The existence, which by its guilt has not reached self-being, summons itself to remember the self, to free itself to a self, to come from 'unreality' to the 'reality' of existence." In other words, in Buber's view, Heidegger is trying to explain human existence without any kind of other-person-hood involved in it. I would agree with Buber. Heidegger's exposition is somewhat frustrating to read, precisely because it uses terms (conscience, guilt) that ordinarily presuppose interpersonal relations — but without any such relations anywhere in sight.[62] To the contrary, Buber continues,

> This presence before which I am placed changes its form, its appearance, its revelation, they are different from myself, often terrifyingly different, and different from what I expected, often terrifyingly different." ...It is not my existence which calls to me, but the being which is not I.

Buber invokes the tradition in contrast to Heidegger:

> "This man, as we recognize him in Augustine, in Pascal, in Kierkegaard, seeks a form of being which is not included in the world, that is, he seeks a divine form of being with which,

---

[60] Clearly, the mainstream tradition thinks it is possible, but I leave that as an open question. On the rabbinic side, Curtis Franks advises great caution.

[61] Buber, *Between Man and Man*, 165, § 2.

[62] See *Being and Time* Division II, chapter 2, §§ 55–60, esp. § 58.

2.9 Martin Buber

> solitary as he is, he can communicate; he stretches his hands out beyond the world to meet this form."[63]

That, of course, is the central theme of the present chapter, and it is found in many more witnesses than just the ones Buber names. Buber quotes Heidegger:

> Further, "Real life together is the first thing to arise out of the real self-being of resolution." Thus it looks as though Heidegger fully knew and acknowledged that a relation to others is essential.[64]

The appearance in Heidegger is misleading, and is typical. Heidegger seems to acknowledge interpersonhood, but he has merely bumped into it and not investigated further. Buber continues:

> But this is not actually the case. For the relation of solicitude which is all he considers cannot *as such* be an essential relation, since it does not set a man's life in direct relation with the life of another, but only one man's solicitous help in relation with another man's lack and need of it.

Buber continues, and touches the nerve of the problem:

> In its essence solicitude does not come from mere co-existence with others, as Heidegger thinks, but from essential, direct, whole relations between man and man ...

He names relationships out of which there could arise an essential interpersonal relatedness as best he can without spotting the mistake on page 12. Human persons have stakes in each other's existence, but there are many ways that happens and canvassing them exhaustively is impossible. Buber restates the critique:

> In man's existence with man it is not solicitude, but the essential relation, which is primordial.... In *mere* solicitude man remains essentially with himself, even if he is moved with extreme pity; in action and help he inclines towards the other, but the barriers of his own being are not thereby breached; he makes his assistance, not his self, accessible to the other....[65]

---

[63] Buber, *Between Man and Man*, 167, § 3.
[64] Buber, *Between Man and Man*, 169, § 5. There is no citation to Heidegger.
[65] Buber, *Between Man and Man*, 170.

Then Buber tries to show some of what Heidegger has left out:

> In an essential relation, on the other hand, the barriers of individual being are in fact breached and a new phenomenon appears which can appear only in this way: one life open to another — not steadily, but so to speak attaining its extreme reality only from point to point, yet also able to acquire a form in the continuity of life; the other becomes present not merely in the imagination or feeling, but in the depths of one's substance, so that one experiences the mystery of the other being in the mystery of one's own. The two participate in one another's lives in very fact, not psychically, but ontically.

Ontically? Ontologically? Ontically because first ontologically? More, in a sort of summary:

> Existence is completed in self-being; there is no ontic way beyond this for Heidegger. What Feuerbach pointed out, that the individual does not have the essence of man in himself, that man's essence is contained in the unity of man with man, has entirely failed to enter Heidegger's philosophy. For him the individual has the essence of man in himself and brings it to existence by becoming a "resolved" self. Heidegger's self is *a closed system*.[66]

In contrast to a closed system, in the anthropology presented here, a human being is neither closed nor a system: it is ontologically constituted by involvements with other people, not all of which can be tracked down. In a real sense I do not and cannot fully know who I am — I am not in control, not even of myself. For Kierkegaard, anxiety arises from the human-God relation; for Heidegger,

> anxiety and dread ... become essential as anxiety about the growth of self-being and dread lest it be missed.... In his anxiety and dread Kierkegaard's man stands "alone before God,"[67] Heidegger's man stands before himself and nothing

---

[66] Buber, *Between Man and Man*, 171.

[67] In the task Buber set for himself, he merely wanted to criticize Heidegger, and did so in exposing what Heidegger did with his sources in Kierkegaard, without also correcting Kierkegaard. For the record, I do not agree with Kierkegaard that we are individuals alone before God; we meet God (or ultimate reality, or whatever) always as persons involved in other persons. H. Richard Niebuhr would have cited George Herbert Mead at this point. Some of this was emphasized to me by Alexander Blair in the 1980s.

else, and — since in the last resort one cannot stand before oneself — he stands in his anxiety and dread before nothing. ... In Kierkegaard's world there is a *Thou* spoken with the very being to the other person ... In Heidegger's world there is no such *Thou*, no true *Thou* spoken from being to being, spoken with one's own being. One does not say this *Thou* to the man for whom one is merely solicitous.[68]

2.10 John Zizioulas

It was John Zizioulas who led me to Martin Buber's comments on Heidegger. His own project extended to Christology and the Trinity, subjects beyond the ambitions of the present work. Buber places a person "in the between" of persons, a phrasing that is suggestive enough, but may be hard to work with. Zizioulas may be a little more helpful. "The Person is otherness in communion and communion in otherness."[69] The theme is repeated often. Persons exist only in relation to other persons. His adversary is the Western instinct for the "ontological priority of the 'self' over the 'other'."[70] By contrast to that mainstream idea, "In personhood there is no 'self,' for in it every 'self' exists only in being affirmed as 'other' by an 'other', not by *contrasting* itself with some 'other'.[71] Much of what Zizioulas surrounds these remarks with is an inquiry into the changing meanings of οὐσια, *substantia*, ὑπόστασις, and above all, πρόσωπον and its translations. They were central in the changing understanding of persons and personhood on the way to a Chalcedonian Christology and an explanation of the Trinity. The East and the West accomplished that task somewhat differently, and that controversy is more than the present inquiry needs.

Briefly, and following Nédoncelle (whom Zizioulas cites as source),[72] more than a half-dozen Greek words could stand for a human being in various aspects and contexts, but none focused the meaning we have in fourth-century and later discussions of *persons* and *personhood*. Of these,

---

[68] Buber, *Between Man and Man*, 172, greatly condensing a long paragraph in Buber.
[69] Zizioulas, *Communion and Otherness*, 9.
[70] Zizioulas, *Communion and Otherness*, 44.
[71] Zizioulas, *Communion and Otherness*, 55. He cites his own *Being as Communion*, ch. 1, on the Trinity.
[72] Nédoncelle, "Prosopon et persona dans l'antiquité classique." *Revue des sciences religieuses* 22 (1948) 277–299. Cited by Zizioulas, *Being as Communion*, 33, n. 20.

Zizioulas focuses on the three or four named above. Among its functional meanings, ὑπόστασις designates the mode of being of something, and it originally meant οὐσια, or (approximately) substance. Its meaning shifted from οὐσια to πρόσωπον, and πρόσωπον itself was recolored. In Zizioulas's account, πρόσωπον lost its association with theatrical masks and came to mean 'person,' though what 'person' means is itself a matter of some discussion.

> The notion of '*hypostasis*' was for a long time identical with that of 'substance.' As such, it basically served the same purpose as the term 'substance' served since Aristotle, namely to answer the ultimate ontological question: what is it that makes a particular being be itself and thus be at all? Suddenly, however, in the course of the fourth century CE and under the pressure of conditions that are worth studying, the term *hypostasis* ceased to denote 'substance' and became synonymous with that of 'person.' ... But since '*hypostasis*' is identical with personhood and not with substance, it is not in its 'self-existence' but in *communion* that this being is *itself* and thus *is at all*.[73]

Then Zizioulas shows the question he is trying to answer, the position he is trying to fend off:

> Thus, communion does not threaten personal particularity; it is constitutive of it.[74]

His implicit adversary starts with human being as substance in a closed ontology and adds other persons later. Some of the features of an ontology of substance:

> Greek thought in all its variations (Platonic, Aristotelian, etc.) always operated with what we may call a closed ontology. As E. L. Mascall puts it, "for both [Platonic and

---

[73] Zizioulas, *Communion and Otherness*, 213–214.

[74] Zizioulas, *Communion and Otherness*, 214, continuing from the previous quotation. The tension between communion and otherness is a repeated theme, and it could be put differently in the terms with which we saw human interinvolvements in the initial critique of Heidegger: many persons have stakes or interests in the being of any one particular person, and those interests sometimes conflict. In passing, that conflict of interests is one of the origins of sin.

2.10 John Zizioulas

Aristotelian thought] every being had a nicely rounded-off nature which contained implicitly everything that the being could ever become... What Greek thought could not have tolerated... would have been the idea that a being could become more perfect in its kind by acquiring some characteristic which was not implicit in its nature before."[75]

For what it is worth, this Greek instinct is at the root of what will later become the systems ontologies of the modern natural sciences. Personhood does not have a systems ontology, even if the material substrate of a particular human individual does.[76]

What I would like to extract from Zizioulas's comments is merely that being a person is primordially a matter of interpersonal relations. This he says many times.

As a person you exist as long as you love and are loved.[77]

This restates the amendment to Heidegger's definition of human being above in section 2.1: to be a person is to interpersonate, primordially. To interpersonate *well* is to love. There are, of course, other ways to interpersonate. In another place, and against a certain kind of individualism,

On the contrary, being a person is basically different from being an individual or 'personality' in that the person cannot be conceived in itself as a static entity, but only as it *relates to*.[78]

Note that in Zizioulas's language, the person "relates to," without saying to *whom*: interpersonating is something we do (or something we be) primordially, logically whether or not particular other persons are present here and now. He expands the point in his footnote no. 12:

The understanding of the person as a *relational* category in our time has marked a sharp contrast with the Boethian individualistic tradition.

He sets himself apart from the contemporary mainstream, which takes consciousness and individuality as the primary ontological features of human personhood.[79]

---

[75] Zizioulas, *Communion and Otherness*, 208, n. 3. The quotation from Mascall is from *The Openness of Being*, 246.

[76] Some of this was explored under other terms in Porter, *Living in Spin*, chapter 3.

[77] Zizioulas, *Communion and Otherness*, 167.

[78] Zizioulas, *Communion and Otherness*, 212.

[79] Zizioulas, *Communion and Otherness*, 210, 212, n. 12, and 224, n. 26.

2.11   A Tentative Synthesis

The synthesis that follows is tentative and preliminary. The sequence of chapters so far has been about language, then personhood, and next two chapters will repeat that sequence: chapter 3 has more about language, and chapter 4 will develop interpersonhood a little more. For what it's worth, I don't think any synthesis could be comprehensive, and that is in the nature of human personhood: it is always open. Readers may find important ideas that are not here. That said, let us attempt to pull from this chapter a perspective on human personhood: It is interpersonal from its beginnings.

Most of this chapter was a tour through various philosophers who have recognized the interpersonal character of human life. Section 2.2, on the sociology of knowledge, gave us a somewhat abstract overview and typology. For concrete examples, consider relationships between people, especially institutional relationships such as friendship, marriage, family, work, economics, property, contracts, and all the private-sector organizations that we use to shape our lives. And government. Why is it that we need a society in which some tell others what to do? Why is *power* so necessary to the functioning of a society and provision of life for individuals? Put this at the third or concrete and particular level of interpersonation, because it is the most obvious and also the most superficial. Beneath the third level will lie a second level, in which human existence is related to other persons, but not to *particular* other persons, though possible other persons are always in the existential vicinity. Beneath the second level will lie a first and primordial level in which interpersonation is possible, as it were, beyond other persons.

To proceed from the third level to the second, consider things like texts which are written for other people but not *particular* other people: they are open works, accessible to anybody. In that openness they show interpersonation present as such, despite the lack of any particular others. Paul Ricoeur traced the same development for human action when he took text as model for action.[80] Action gets "saved" when it is transformed into something open to anyone. (This is also a step on the way to placing action in history, though such was not one of his goals in that essay.) This second level of interpersonation deals with others as possible or virtual others. It undertakes projects that are open to any one, actual or potential, real or vir-

---

[80] Ricoeur, "The Model of Text."

tual. Any act, any engagement with reality is open to others in this sense. We have come to *meaning*, as such: meaning is always *sharable* with others, whether or not it is *actually* shared. At this point we have paralleled two of Thomas Sheehan's steps in *Making Sense of Heidegger* in his exposition of the three levels of truth, ἀλήθεια-3, -2, and -1. The deepest and most primordial (hence numbered 1, not 3) is about the openness of the world to human understanding.

In Sheehan's example, to inquire about ἀλήθεια-1 is to ask why the world is intelligible at all. The problem is that the question already *presupposes* that the world is intelligible. What Sheehan does not emphasize is that intelligibility itself already presupposes other people, *to* whom and *with* whom meaning can be shared. It is not possible to get "behind" or "before" either the intelligibility of the world or the other persons, both real and possible, who participate in that intelligibility.

The primordial level simply has to be accepted; it cannot be derived because it is presupposed in any inquiry about anything at all in the world — and especially about the world itself, as a whole. Perhaps it can be redescribed but that is not the same as deriving it from something even more primordial. We can say a little about it, in the sense that it is possible to know *some* of what we have presupposed.

Come back to Heidegger's definitions of human being and apply some of what we have seen about interpersonation in this chapter. There are two definitions. In corrected form, the first is that human being is the sort of being that has a stake in its own being — and in whom other such beings also have a stake. The second is that human being is the sort of being (ambiguous in regard to singular or plural) that understands being. In the last phrase, to understand being is to have a world.[81] Heidegger himself said that in engaging a tool we meet the other people for whom also it is a useful tool. It is odd that this was not generalized. In engaging any phenomenon at all, whether a person or a thing, we meet also the other people for whom that person or thing makes sense. To make sense of people or things is a corporate project. It is still a corporate project even when we face another person who also makes sense of *us*.

We have stakes in the being of every person. What stakes? Meaning, making sense of the world. What does it mean to make sense of the world?

---

[81] What we can say about the world apart from our understanding of it is precisely nothing, so we keep silence. Both Sheehan's commentary and Wittgenstein's ending in the *Tractatus* emphasize this.

To see the possibilities for living, for being, for mattering to other people, and in the end, for bringing a life to some sort of closure. Everybody agrees that it is possible to live well or poorly, though we disagree about *how* to do that. Here in passing, for what it is worth, is one of the roots of disappointing behavior (i.e., sin).

Is this objective? No, objectivity is not possible, but responsibility is. Responsibility to whom? To a community of competents, whose judgement one accepts as mattering, even when it is wrong.[82] And beyond any such community of competents? In the present inquiry, we answer not to Platonic ideals but to what an idealized community *should* say. In effect, we interpersonate after all other persons are exhausted. Real universals are a way of conducting that interpersonation while covering up what we are doing.[83] There is nothing there, and it is that Nothing to whom we appeal and in whom we trust. The difference between objectivity and responsibility is that objectivity hides engagement with other people while responsibility acknowledges it prominently.

Could we have evolved differently and with a different relation to ultimate reality? Obviously. Many have speculated about such contingencies, but let me name only one. All animals have stakes in the being of other life, both conspecifics and otherwise, but humans, language capable life, seem to understand this better than any other species we know of. One contributing cause is the fact that we are born unfinished, and the last years of brain formation take place in a social context: we are not physically mature until we are socialized.

---

[82] Porter, *Living in Spin*, sections 5.4.3 and 5.4.4.

[83] This is not to advocate nominalism instead; my own instincts tend rather to moderate realism, which strikes me as a position outside of the circle of realism and nominalism.

Chapter 3

Language, Self, World, Action

3.1 Getting Into Language

We opened with the ambiguity of language in the first chapter, and met interpersonhood in the second. It is time to say more about language. Peter Berger once said, in effect, that language, self, and the world are a package, and language is the carrier of the package. "Language is both the most important content and the most important instrument of socialization."[1]

The Western philosophical tradition has always been aware of language and its features but the understanding of language has changed greatly in the last century and a half. There have been other periods of change but this one is what we have to deal with now.

A re-understanding of language usually provokes a time of philosophical crisis. The "how it works" of language gets revised, and responses to the instigating challenge range from trust to distrust and from naive to a critical new understanding. Often distrust (the old understanding has failed) takes forms such as materialism, nominalism, or empiricism,[2] falling back on what is visibly demonstrable. New trust can be hard-won, but with it can come a recovery of some sort of realism, whether idealist, critical, hermeneutical, or something else of the sort.

Things began in nineteenth century mathematics, when George Boole started exploring logic. That became a communal inquiry focusing on the predicate logic of Gottlob Frege and parallel developments in set theory

---
[1] Berger and Luckmann, *The Social Construction of Reality*, 133.
[2] This insight originally came from Doris Myers and W. M. Urban. See Myers, *C. S. Lewis in Context*, 1. She cites Urban, *Language and Reality*, 21–24.

that were put on a rigorous basis by Ernst Zermelo and Abraham Fraenkel among others. They set much of the agenda for mathematics in the twentieth century. This was the first progress in formal logic since Aristotle, and it opened up problems that Aristotelian logic could handle clumsily at best. At first, it looked as if the re-founding of mathematics on the ground of set theory would in principle answer all questions and provide the kind of certainty that the Western philosophical heart has always been tempted to seek.[3] Then Russell and others discovered that there was no set of all sets, and that was only the first of many disturbing paradoxes at the roots of mathematics. Exhaustive certainty is not given to mathematics. The names Gödel, Kleene, Church, Rosser, and Turing tell the story, but it is not our story.

Change in mathematics was accompanied at some distance by a new perspective on ordinary language itself. I don't know where to find a history of the philosophy of language before the twentieth century, but it must have included grammar, which probably meant taking Latin (and Latin grammar) as the model for all other languages. Such was the European academic history. A casual search on the Net easily demonstrates that what started in a few texts in Plato and grammarians has grown to something vast, touching every area of philosophy, and every relation of human being and human mind to others and to the world. Change and significant breakthroughs came with many thinkers. John Ellis names Saussure, Peirce, and Wittgenstein as chief among them, and observes that they were not aware of each other's work.[4] Some of their readers understood (or oversimplified) fragments and turned those fragments into a handsome living peddling them either as solutions to all problems or as proof that all problems in the end have no solution. I myself have no use for theories of everything or anti-theories of nihilism, but my own knowledge is limited in ways that are all too similar to those Ellis surveys. So the reader is cautioned. My ambitions and abilities are more modest: a few observations about the place of language in relating to the world that may help us make sense of unanswerable questions, the threshold of transcendence.

Given these cautions, it may still help to note a few of the mistakes that Ellis calls out.[5] The recurrent theme is that language is not first or

---

[3] There are non-Western traditions of formal logic, but they are still new material to Western inquiry. In the sense of Rémi Brague (*Eccentric Culture*), the West always hopes to learn from other cultures, but we are still beginners.

[4] Ellis, *Language, Thought, and Logic*, 4.

[5] We have seen them already, in *The Accountant's Tale*, 192, section 9.1.

3.1 Getting Into Language

originally a way to describe the world, with its parts (words) denoting or referring to things in the world. Language underwrites being-in-the-world,[6] but that is to get ahead of our story. Let me summarize only the three commonest mistakes in the philosophy of language that Ellis gives us.

> The first of these missteps can be stated very simply. It is the assumption that the purpose of language is communication.... It immediately misdirects all subsequent effort in linguistic theory.[7]

The second is

> the assumption that descriptive words like *square* or *cat* are simpler and easier to understand than evaluative words like *good* and that the former are therefore more basic and thus a better model to take for understanding how language works.

He continues, with Chomsky in mind as adversary:

> [T]he assumption ... that science begins by taking the clear cases and then generalizes from them to formulate the principles that are used to deal with the difficult cases.... The movement of thought is assumed to be from simple to complex.

The third error assumes

> that the verbal categories of language serve to group like things together.... the exact reverse is the important truth for linguistic theory: verbal categories group *unlike* things.

Later in response to the third error, he says that

> we grasp the essence of the process of categorization only when we see it as the grouping together of things that are not the same in order that they will *count* as the same (p. 24).

To "count" as the same is to bump into the humans *for whom* they count as the same — we deal with some dissimilar things in similar ways; that

---
[6] We borrow Heidegger's phrase, but do not limit ourselves to Heidegger's meaning.
[7] These are from Ellis, *Language, Thought, and Logic*, 15–16.

is part of coping in the world. Heidegger was not named but could have been.

Exploration of language at the beginning of the twentieth century uncovered enough problems, these three among them, to shake confidence in the reliability of language. Many simply reaffirmed the assumptions that Ellis demurs from, in a reactionary retreat into the many forms of logicism: something simple, a kind of nominalism, as Myers' comments on Urban observed above. The logical form of that move was to restrict language to functions that could be expressed in a predicate calculus, where language could be controlled, without noticing problems that turned up in the predicate calculus itself. Not spelled out was the obvious use of such a program: to get control over our own being-in-the-world and defend against ambiguity, uncertainty, and insecurity through control of language.

The philosophy of language is not the only witness against platonist (and nominalist) certainties that we all inherited from the modern period. We have met another in the sociology of knowledge (sec. 2.2). It assumes for its own necessary purposes that all knowledge is a social construction. Many took that as an entry into nihilism, meaninglessness for lack of real knowledge. But instead of nihilism (as in deconstruction), it is possible to ask, If everything is a social construction, why are some social constructions better than others? (And which ones?) That problem was solved before the latter-day nihilists came into flower, notably in the work of Thomas Kuhn and others.[8] It is possible to compare and judge competing paradigms without having a neutral standpoint from which to judge. Nominalism and nihilism come from disappointed Platonism, giving up the platonist solutions but not the platonist problem. Nihilism results from an inability to live with ambiguity, uncertainty, and theory-change in history. But that is precisely our task: to live in a world that is ambiguous, one in which we have at best incomplete and uncertain knowledge. We cope. We are not platonists and also not disappointed platonists (nominalists or nihilists).

Yet more testimony against platonist certainties is the structure of interpretation that came out in phenomenology and hermeneutics. That structure, in the "hermeneutical circle," could seem from a platonist/nominalist point of view to be vicious, to undercut the possibility of reliable knowl-

---

[8] I have usually cited Alasdair MacIntyre's work, e.g., *Whose Justice, Which Rationality?*, 362. John Ellis says that Charles Sanders Peirce anticipated Kuhn, so things may be more interesting than our inherited myths would have one believe.

3.1 Getting Into Language

edge. On that reading, it would be yet one more excuse for nihilism. George Steiner, thinking as a literary critic, saw it as the entry into what goes by the name of "deconstruction," just such a movement of despair. He finds the roots of this latter-day nihilism late in the nineteenth century, and the root issue is language and trust in language (or not), just as Doris Myers remarked (p. 55 above). There were many kinds of skepticism before the twentieth century, but they all accepted the validity of language as a medium in which to prosecute their skeptical complaints against their adversaries. That presupposition of trust in language as a medium of expression failed a century ago, as we have seen in the events briefly recounted above. Steiner remarks,

> But the decisive point has been this: until the crisis of the meaning of meaning which began in the late nineteenth century, even the most astringent skepticism, even the most subversive of anti-rhetorics, remained committed to language. It knew itself to be 'in trust' to language. Pyrrhonism, which is the classical font and paradigm of Western skepticism, does not question its own right, its own capacity, to put its case in the form of articulate, grammatically organized propositions.[9]

He continues a little later,

> [S]kepticism accepted the contract with language.... It is my belief that this contract is broken for the first time, in any thorough and consequent sense, in European, Central European and Russian culture and speculative consciousness during the decades from the 1870s to the 1930s. *It is this break of the covenant between word and world which constitutes one of the very few genuine revolutions of spirit in Western history and which defines modernity itself*.[10]

It is fair to observe that the contract with language implicitly took language to be a way to get conceptual control over being-in-the-world and to resolve all ambiguities. After all, to cope with some situation in life is to seek control, at least for a day; never spelled out was the obvious hope to get control permanently, at least in theory if not in practice. To those goals

---

[9] Steiner, *Real Presences*, 92. Note how he focuses language in *propositions*. We return to that below.

[10] Steiner, *Real Presences*, 92–93. Italics in the original.

I would add a desire in some measure to evade or shield oneself from the challenges of other people. But platonist certainty and control are not available, and they are not our task. Our task is to understand ambiguity, to understand coping *without* being in control. Theologians going all the way back to the Bible would have recognized that as part of creaturehood and recognized attempts to get out of the limitations of creaturehood as one of the roots of sin. Still, until recently, even these theological cautions trusted language, as did skepticism, as a medium in which to conduct their distrusts.

> That which necessarily underwrites such recognitions and valuations is nothing more nor less than the myth, now glaringly untenable, of divine guarantee.... The issue is, quite simply, that of the meaning of meaning as it is re-insured by the postulate of the existence of God. "In the beginning was the Word."[11]

We are up against what H. Richard Niebuhr called the void that is the failure of all our causes, and at this point in the logic, we have not yet come to terms with that void, we have not yet come to trust it. Nevertheless, the heart cries out! To question language is to question the ontological constitution of human being; to reject language is to reject our own human being; to take offense at language is to take offense at our own humanity. Do we have to take offense at our own being? Do we have to take offense at the limitations of language? It may well be that our actions can always be *construed* as taking offense, but that is not the only possibility. Here the ambiguity of language is not just the problem we instinctively take offense at, it is the only hope for a solution. If we are really to embrace the void that undermines all our causes, then we are left vulnerable, without any supports, like a cartoon character who has just run off a cliff and now has only air for support. We are dependent on grace; good theology acknowledges that and so gives up any sort of triumphalism. At this point, the mind, as Aquinas once said, rests in a kind of "thick darkness,"[12] after he has followed pseudo-Dionysius and the *via negativa* in removing "existence" from God. We know we will be found wrong. We *hope* for that finding, and we trust that it will bring "salvation" rather than confound

---

[11] Steiner, *Real Presences*, 120.

[12] In *Super Sententiarum*, 1.8.1.1 ad 4, "haec est quaedam caligo, in qua Deus habitare dicitur."

us.[13]

So let us look again at the features of language that define us and our relation to reality, ultimate and otherwise. Language is the medium that gives us being-in-the-world (sec. 3.2). Language gives us the ontological constitution of action, human and otherwise (sec. 3.3). Language gives us selfhood along with worldhood (sec. 3.3). Language has powers far beyond mere propositions (sec. 3.4).

3.2 Language and World

That language gives us a world is a glib summary of a vast inheritance. I hope we can manage with only a few features of it.

We need two things: In the first, language gives us persons, things, and events far away, in the past and the future, the actual and the possible. The second is an existential interpersonhood that comes from the interpersonal structure of language itself: it is shared, it is always potentially spoken *to* other persons. The second we have seen in chapter 2. At present, it is the first we are interested in.

Persons, events, and things in the world are a context in which we live. Heidegger called that living "Being-in-the-World"; Hubert Dreyfus glossed it as *coping*. To live is to cope. To cope is to see and exploit the possibilities for living. Many things in the world make sense to us, and we can bring them to language — or better, bring them out into the open with language. Sometimes the language we use can withstand criticism, but sometimes it touches the phenomena only in the way that the phlogiston theory really was about combustion.[14] Sometimes we have only poetry, metaphor, irony (and maybe even myths), especially when we are dealing with human and existential phenomena. Sometimes we come up against what doesn't make sense, what resists our understanding and our languaging. Heidegger called this the "uncanny." The German word is *unheimlich*, which one might translate literally as not-at-home-ness. Edward Hobbs defined theology as using language to make a home for man in the universe, and so the uncanny can serve to remind us how precarious our socially constructed homes are.

Like Heidegger, we turn our questioning about the world back on the questioner (ourselves), for we are as much a mystery to ourselves as the

---

[13] This was the Exposure in the series Exposure, Limitation, and Need.

[14] Phlogiston really is a scientific theory of combustion; it just happens to be wrong.

world is. One mode of that reflexive questioning is the attempt to bring into the light at least some of our presuppositions.

Thomas Sheehan proposed a coherent summary of Heidegger's project as a whole. Central to the structure of human understanding that resulted was an analysis of three stages of truth: truth as correspondence, truth as the showing-themselves of things in the world, and simply the intelligibility of the world at all. The last is the clearing in which things can show themselves, even before we try to articulate in language what they are and how they work. The most primordial stage Sheehan called $\dot{\alpha}\lambda\dot{\eta}\theta\epsilon\iota\alpha$-1. It can only be accepted but not further analyzed because it is itself always already presupposed in any inquiry about itself.

Why do we even ask about the "causes" of the intelligibility of the world? The meaning of "why?" has here changed from its usage in ordinary intramundane contexts. In ordinary usage, "why such-and-such" effectively means tell me how to cope with such-and-such, tell me how such-and-such fits into the world. In asking about $\dot{\alpha}\lambda\dot{\eta}\theta\epsilon\iota\alpha$-1 we ask something like "why me?" Why are we here in a world, this world? Questioning cannot reach outside this world to grasp a larger context in which this world and human life in it could be made sense of. The possibility of asking such a question is not just a peculiar and paradoxical feature of the logic of language, although it is that too. It manifests a human existential bewilderment toward selfhood and existence. It is a mystery, not a puzzle, though there are puzzles enough about the mystery. Mysteries are unanswerable questions.

3.3 Language, Narrative, Action

To understand the world as a context for living is to understand the world as a context for action. When asked what language does, we instinctively reach for words that refer to "things," i.e., solid bodies in a transparent medium. But that is not most of what we do with language — mostly, we talk about *actions*. "Things" appear insofar as they fit into talk about actions. Heidegger is not as helpful about action as he was about being-in-the-world. In *Living in Spin* I tried to fill in some of what Heidegger did not ask about, building on resources in Paul Ricoeur. In *Spin*, action turned out to be always already related to narrative, and thus rooted in language.

In *Living in Spin* I said that an act happens when some contingency affects someone's interests and is narratable (p. 5). The definition is circular, but it could be amended to say merely that narrative brings to language contingencies that affect persons' interests. Many features of the language of action appeared in that book but two should stand out before all the others. We said above (with Heidegger) that language *gathers*; here, language *selects*: narrative brings into being the actions it recounts because it selects from all the "motions" in the world the ones that matter to the narrative editor. In the second place, language of action is ambiguous, simply because contingencies and interests are both already ambiguous. In other words, there is a hermeneutically circular relation between narrative and action. They are constituted together. To the second feature, I would add that we have not entirely learned how to live with ambiguity, how to make sense of the world in ways that integrate its ambiguity rather than fleeing from it or denying its ambiguity. In the end, I think we will come to see ambiguity as the pivotal condition of a solution rather than as the problem.[15]

We emphasize the hearers of narrative, both real and virtual. Narrative is meant for readers or hearers. Narrative shapes actions, narrative shapes lives. Narrative matters to people because it shapes their lives. When I took Jim McClendon's ethics course, he always assigned an autobiography and invited students to ask whether the author, the autobiographer, came to terms with his life honestly and responsibly. The key word is "responsibly." Responsibly to whom? As Paul Ricoeur labored in "The Model of Text," an act of any interest gets detached from its original circumstances and becomes open to anyone. (That, too, is a process of transformation of narratives.)

Why do bystanders (or readers, in the case of text) have any interest in the acts described? "Interest" has at least two senses — the superficial one, in which a story is interesting or dull, and the deeper sense, in which it is relevant or not. For a story to be relevant, the reader has to have *stakes* in the story. That can happen in more than one way. The story can justify or challenge the reader's life and circumstances fairly directly. Journalism and history curricula in America today are loaded with such applications and with disputes about them. A story can simply tell how the present came from the past. The world after World War II was shaped by that war, and to understand the present world requires understanding how it came to be.[16] To understand the twentieth century requires understanding what

---

[15] Some of this is in later sections on ambiguity and analogy.
[16] Critics of modern education marvel at how students get along quite happily without any such knowledge.

came before it, and so-on, further back. Historians, professional or amateur, usually fall in love with some particular period and then specialize — which raises more questions than are usually noticed. For the rest of history, the context before and after, has been delegated to other specialists. It may simply be accepted as imperfectly known and understood. It is that way with biblical history, much of which is inaccessible to us. What does that do to the status of biblical religion today? We (or scholars) have recovered much of the history of biblical religion, history that would have seemed impossible two hundred years ago, and we think we are richer for it.

There is another way in which readers have stakes in a narrative. We can see this within narratives, especially those that tell more than one story in parallel. Shakespeare often puts a minor story into the unfolding of the main story, as when Kent's sons provide a foil for Lear's daughters. The key is the concept of a foil: the foil by its similarities and differences tells us something about the central story. (This happens in the Bible also, but it is seldom noticed.) If we live in an ontology in which the narratives are constitutive of the things they narrate, then we are dealing with ontological foils (a term used in *Spin*). In effect, when I, as a reader, read the tale of so-and-so, I am learning something about who and what I am, because the tale supplies foils that have ontological effects on all other stories, including my own. We are back to ambiguity. For such effects cannot be nailed down exhaustively, they cannot even be tracked down and enumerated, and even when they are seen, they can be interpreted in many ways. Note that the tale usually has one main character (rather than many); that is the way that movies are structured. Most books follow the pattern. So when I consider a story, I am dealing with some character who dealt with his (or her) circumstances; I take lessons from his strategies, successes, and failures. This is an instance of what we saw in chapter 2 on personhood and its roots in interpersonhood. My being is constituted (in part) by involvements with other persons beyond count.

Selfhood has many features and aspects, and narrative is only one, whether narrative by the self in view or by others. Language is the original link between a self and the world, and it is one original link to other people (touch is another, and one the few that are more primordial than language). We spend much of our time telling stories about ourselves and others. It gets tacitly assumed but never spelled out that a life has *one* story, whether told or not, but people tell many stories about themselves. Biographers tell one. Sometimes the subject collects his stories in one, as in an autobiography; but more often people do not. Nonetheless, we easily assume that a life has a narrative coherence as *one* story, whether it is told or not. It is easy to tell partial stories about a life, my involvements of one kind in one story, leaving other involvements for other stories. Maybe we *seek* and *construct* a unifying narrative in a quest for some sort of "narrative salvation." In the myths of Judgement Day, it is that narrative coherence that gets judged — and in that appraisal, gives selfhood to the self in view.

3.4 Language Beyond Propositions

The notion of a reality beyond language can have at least two meanings: realities beyond propositions, or beyond language simply. There is more to language than propositions. Only if figurative language, irony, and expressive language are ruled out of order can all engagement with the world be confined to propositions.[17] Perhaps one could call the two meanings of reality beyond language *apophatic* and *radically* apophatic. In the first, the "phatic" beyond which there is still meaning is what can be told in propositions. That is within the meanings of $\phi\eta\mu\iota$, from which comes $\dot{\alpha}\pi\acute{o}\phi\alpha\sigma\iota\varsigma$, denial. It carries overtones of simultaneous denial and assertion. $\Phi\eta\mu\iota$ itself is given as "to say, speak, tell; to express one's opinion or thoughts; to be of opinion, believe, think, imagine" (Liddell and Scott). More radically, as $\dot{\alpha}\pi\acute{o}\phi\alpha\sigma\iota\varsigma$, by contraction of $\dot{\alpha}\pi\acute{o}\phi\alpha\nu\sigma\iota\varsigma$, from $\phi\alpha\acute{\iota}\nu\omega$, it can mean virtually the opposite: a sentence, decision (again, Liddell and Scott). Both are akin to expression in language but not always in propositions. It is sometimes said that language is capable of "pointing" to things that are quite beyond its power to express. That is tricky and usually carries a risk of being mistaken for expressing the inexpressible, as when "pointing to" is mistaken for monstration and that is further mistaken for demonstration. Demonstration would violate at least two canons of method: it would appear to be proof,[18] and it would suck the transcendent into the grasp of reasoning about the intramundane. Very comforting, but in bad faith.

There are traditional ways of dealing with these problems, but the logic

---

[17] We are frustrated when we bump into a reality that cannot be captured in propositions, and it is easy to reassert propositions by presupposition, simply by arguing about the reality in question. To argue is to argue over propositions.

[18] See section 5.2 in this book and the discussions of proofs in *The Accountant's Tale*.

of the present inquiry is somewhat different. Traditionally, in "cataphatic" theology (among its other names), the theologian and believer predicates attributes of God positively, and then in another voice, "apophatic" theology denies those same predicates of God. This in its compound structure is a way of expressing the fact that language fails to grasp God. William Placher notes the premodern tradition[19]:

> ...before the seventeenth century, most Christian theologians were struck by the mystery, the wholly otherness of God, and the inadequacy of any human categories as applied to God. That earlier view never completely disappeared, but in the seventeenth century philosophers and theologians increasingly thought they could talk clearly about God.

and

> Rather than explaining how all categories break down when applied to God, they set the stage for talking about transcendence as one of the definable properties God possesses — a quality we could understand and that many writers today could then come to find deeply unattractive. In that sense, transcendence got domesticated, and theology suffered as a result.[20]

They knew that human categories fail to grasp God, but human categories are necessary nonetheless. What is seldom remarked in the traditional method of apophatic or negative theology is that the logical right to use the term 'God' was taken for granted. After all, the Name appears in the liturgy and inherited texts, biblical and otherwise. We are familiar with speaking both to and of God, hence the ease of taking the term for granted. What is not noticed is that the term 'God' is ambiguous, and despite the best of intentions, it can be heard first to nominalize and then to hypostatize or reify its referent. In other words, it can be heard to *refer*, and that meaning can never wholly be removed from it, not even in the method of the via negativa.

The logic in the present book differs from the tradition above. We do not start by taking for granted the term 'God' and then asking what

---

[19] We have seen this in more detail in *The Accountant's Tale*, in section 6.1.

[20] Placher, *The Domestication of Transcendence*, 6–7. There is more discussion of Placher in *The Accountant's Tale*, section 6.1.

it means. We started with philosophical anthropology: human beings are constituted as always already other-person related, and we other-relate in everything we know or do in the world, and we do so even after all the other persons in the world have been accounted for. That was the point of chapter 2. Nevertheless, more cautions are in order.

To start with anthropology was the method of Friedrich Schleiermacher, and so we court some risks with this logic. I don't much care for Schleiermacher's solutions to his problems, because he doesn't appear to have ever recovered any real transcendence. People other than me have remarked as much. But few people in this world are wrong about everything, and Schleiermacher was not one of them. He was correct to look beyond the inherited dualism that travels with modern supernaturalism (Humean "miracles").[21] The challenge is to recover a sense of transcendence without a supernatural dualism, and few think that the tradition stemming from Schleiermacher succeeded in that. Among the mistakes in his method one assumes that it is possible to start with the intramundane and derive what transcendence is available from it. To the contrary, I think transcendence of some better sort is always already presupposed. The task then is to show that presupposition — without drawing transcendence into the intramundane. That drawing can happen in at least two ways, as already noted above: by appearing to "prove" transcendence or by talking about it with a logic appropriate to the intramundane. The first is in bad faith (as noted more than once), and the second violates a Chalcedonian method. The trouble with a naive version of a Chalcedonian method is that it too easily speaks of the transcendent in ambiguous ways that invite the same familiar kinds of trouble. The transcendent is treated as an invisible extension of the intramundane.

3.5 Unanswerable Questions

We first saw unanswerable questions in sec. 2.6, "Beyond Answerable Questions." It is time to return to them. Language beyond propositions takes us to transcendence when we come by way of unanswerable questions. Many examples can be found; then we can attempt some generaliza-

---

[21] The risk we court here is that there might be yet other alternatives to the modern supernatural dualism than the one we have here modified from Schleiermacher. A classic pitfall is to reject someone's solutions without correcting his problematic. We attempt to correct the problematic; success or failure is another matter.

tions about their character.

Consider a few examples.

> Why me?
> Why did this have to happen to me?
> Why do I have to die?
> Why is there a world and not nothing at all?

The first two can be asked in both grief and rejoicing. To respond with "These things just happen" is to change the meaning of the question. It rejects answers and deals with the questions silently in some other way. To ask about mortality is exemplary of asking about the pains of life. To ask why there is a world appears on second inspection to be incoherent, but on third, it tells us something about being human in a world.

There are lists of basic questions asked in placing human life in its larger context. Some of the necessary parts of a theology:

> Cosmology (the character of the world);
> cosmogony (how the world came about);
> metaphysics (what's real, what's not, and how);
> theological and philosophical anthropology
> theological psychology
> a doctrine of "salvation"
>   (what it would mean to succeed or fail in life);
> an ethics
> an eschatology (what happens to us in the end);
> a "theodicy" (how to explain the pains of life);
> and a soteriology (how to deal with the pains of life).[22]

These are not prima facie unanswerable; theologians do a brisk trade in answering them, even though they lead to unanswerable questions. They are open to dispute, for people disagree about all of them. Here is another list, one that moves a lot closer to the unanswerable:

> Who am I?
> Where have I come from? and
> Where am I going?
> Why is there evil?
> What is there after this life?[23]

---

[22] From Porter, *Where, Now, O Biologists*, 41–42, abbreviated.
[23] *Fides et Ratio*, § 1.

3.5 Unanswerable Questions

The trivial intramundane answers to the first two questions are Andrew Porter and his parents, in Boston, Massachusetts — but that isn't what the questions are really about, and the disquiet with the trivial intramundane answers takes us to unanswerable questions. It is just as D. Z. Phillips said, we ask these questions *after* answers have done all they can, and unless this is seen, the meaning of the questions has been missed.

There are situations in life, or perhaps just phenomena in life, that give rise to unanswerable questions. Some have called them boundary situations, after Karl Jaspers. He himself cited death, suffering, struggle, and guilt.[24] Peter Berger explored another series of phenomena that cry out for some kind of transcendence:[25] Order, play, hope, humor, and grace.[26] They all raise unanswerable questions in a rich and textured way. They are usually not phrased as questions (though they can be, I suppose); they are just phenomena or clearings in which appears something very close to contradictions. Like Stephen Mulhall, we take them not as logical dead-ends but as openings into what it means to be human.

The character of the logic that one eventually comes to stands out in a few examples, and it has attracted inquiry about the basic relation of humans to the world. Consider

What does "means" mean?

Any answer is necessarily circular, because to ask what something means is to presuppose an understanding of "means." Examples of usage may be given, and the one who asks may "get the hang of it," seeing from the examples how to use the concept of meaning, but that is probably the best that can be done. A more concrete instance of this kind of questioning would ask why the world is orderly and intelligible under the aspect of nature.[27] It just is. That has to be accepted if one is to do modern natural science — which bumps into the possibility of *not* doing science. In passing, we may note that even unanswerable questions are voluntary (and so responsible); others may choose differently, and often do. Just because *we* (whoever the "we" is) find them compelling in the form we understand them doesn't mean everybody agrees with "us."

---

[24] Jaspers, *Philosophy*, vol. II, part iii, chapter 7, "Boundary Situations," 178.

[25] Berger, *A Rumor of Angels*.

[26] The last was treated under its opposite, depravity, because he thought it was logically more accessible.

[27] "Sub specie naturae." The question matters in a scientific culture.

Thomas Sheehan in *Making Sense of Heidegger* considered clearings and ἀλήθεια as a phenomenon at the ontological root of human being. To paraphrase, the clearing is part of the constitution of human being, and that is why we can see or tell what anything in the world is; but we cannot answer why there is a clearing *itself*.[28] To ask why the world is intelligible or hospitable is like asking what *means* means. In passing, what goes for meaning goes also for mattering: the world matters to us, and mattering, itself, just has to be accepted. I don't know how to get behind it. Sheehan speaks of a *clearing* in which we can "see" the world and things in it. What he does not emphasize (because Heidegger himself rarely notes it) is that we are never existentially alone in this clearing. That is one of the points of the present book.

Why do we *ask* unanswerable questions? If they are unanswerable, what do they really mean? To ask "why?" about something or other is to ask, "Tell me how my world fits together, with a place in it for me." We push the questioning beyond answerable questions out of a sort of dissatisfaction. It comes from the structure of human being; it is built in, in anxiety and uncanniness especially. To ask "why?" is to try to get out of uncanniness. That is one of its meanings but hardly the only one. The uncanny (in German, Unheimlich or not-at-home-ness) comes upon us when our questioning takes us beyond answers. To ask "why?" is to ask, "Tell me how to be-in-the-world," and that is a little different from asking how my world fits together. It is a demand, but a demand for instructions, and like all questions, it presupposes other persons to whom the questioning is directed. We are always together in our not-at-home-ness.

---

[28] Sheehan, *Making Sense of Heidegger*, 75 and passim.

Chapter 4

Interpersonation Again

4.1 Beyond All Persons

As noted in section 2.11 (p. 52), the chapters so far have alternated between language, personhood, and language. It is time to return to personhood — which is to say interpersonhood.

We have already said that in world-affirming (biblical) religion, we still interpersonate after all other intramundane persons have done all they can. We saw as much in the beginning of sec. 2.6, when D. Z. Phillips observed that when we ask "why?" in a religious sense, we ask after answers have done all they can for us. Ordinary answers are not enough. Chapter 2 brought many witnesses who attest that we are always already related to other persons. In the same way as with Phillips's why-questions, we still interpersonate, beyond all particular and intramundane persons, both real and possible. But why? What is the structure of such a personhood? Why is the "beyond all persons" needed?

The short and slightly snarky answer is that other people have a track record, and it is not entirely reassuring.[1] We answer to other persons. And sometimes they are wrong or worse. We know we do not know all there is to know about the world.

The concepts of both truth and being include the feature that they are not simply made-up. Nor can they be simply declared by everybody else. They are not a matter of majority vote. That would be philosophy speaking, but another voice in philosophy acknowledges that the world as we

---

[1] It is not an answer that I am happy with, for interpersonation as a mode of being in the world has slipped through the fingers (again). Perhaps other writers can do better.

know it is the only world we can know; the world "as it is in itself, independent of human knowing," is a dubious thought-construct. As soon as any of *that* world becomes known, it becomes part of the world as we know it. For what it is worth, included in what we can and do know are many answerable questions that we do not (yet) have answers to. About those things we already know something, namely, that we do not yet know much about them.

One recurrent dispute in philosophy has been about whether the human mind is passive in knowing the world or whether it is active in constructing its understanding of the world.[2] We work in the moderate realist tradition, in which the mind is an agent intellect. That leads us to one presupposition of the sociology of knowledge, that all reality as we know it is a human social construction. But how are we to judge social constructions? Some are better than others, surely? It would be natural to ask whether real reality enters into our social constructions. That way lie the many versions of Platonism, in which reality independent of our knowing it lurks hidden someplace from where it can enter into our approximations of it. (Nominalisms are not far behind, though not entirely in the same way.)

This need not be developed in detail, though some do. I would say that it merely is a way of expressing our trust that there is some truth in our truths, but the meaning of 'truth' has shifted to something more like troth. Whose troth? We have come once again to our own interpersonation beyond all intramundane persons, all created persons in this or any other world.

We have also come to a pattern that Thomas Sheehan found in Heidegger, one in which truth appears in three levels (cf. sec. 2.11). At the most superficial level, in thinking about some phenomenon, we may (or may not) remember the closest other people whom we think ought to validate our conclusions. At the middle level, the other people are there in the background, whether they are noticed or not. At the deepest and most primordial level, our thinking and our relating are relative to other people with whom we share the world; again whether we notice them or not. That relatedness is ontological. It is part of the structure of the being of "the world as we know it."

We trust that reality has in some sense plighted its troth to us. This is

---

[2] See Kenny, "Aquinas and Wittgenstein," where Kenny contrasts moderate realism (for which knowledge is the result of an agent intellect) with various nominalisms (for which the human mind is a passive knower).

a positive answer to a question: You have been thrown into the world; is it a good place? Do you want to trust it? We trust but trust critically: the natural world has no interest in pampering us; indeed, it doesn't care much for us at all. That is the doorway into inquiring beyond just the material and natural world. The pains of life put us on the threshold of transcendence, without compelling *how* that threshold is to be met. Eventually, it became clear that we have access to the world and reality only through our own interpretations; another reason to be cautious and critical. Above all, we know that reality may interpret our social constructions differently from how we ourselves do. When one of our socially constructed interpretations of the world or things in it gets into trouble, we trust that the troubles (Exposure, Limitation, and Need) will bear blessings; indeed, we plead that they wear their blessings on their sleeve. Sometimes they do.

4.2 Stakes in Life

Above, we corrected Heidegger's mistake on page 12 of *Being and Time* to say that human being is the sort of being that has a stake in its own being — and other human beings also have an equiprimordial stake in its being (p. 19 ff. above). But what is a stake? There are many stakes and many ways to conceive and construe the stakes a person and other persons have in his being. So the concept and its referents are ambiguous, and that ambiguity arises because stakes can be characterized only in language. Ambiguity is always already present in the language used to conceive human stakes in life and the world.

To say that A has a stake in X means that A stands to gain or lose from X. X affects the life of A, for better or for worse. How? To some extent, this is at the discretion of the people involved; to some extent, it is not. They can define it as they like, subject to limitations that are not always well understood. A person has a stake in society and in a stable and supportive world. One could say that a person has a stake in his own living, her own being in society and the world. To have a stake in one's own being is to have a stake in one's own selfhood. Selfhood is what I stand to gain or lose. In lesser disappointments, I merely fail to get something that I wanted. Wanted what? Something defined in a narrative. Much of what a self is is constituted in narratives about oneself, told by oneself and by others. But narratives are ambiguous.

What are the stakes that other persons have in one person's being?

Or I in other persons' being? The answer goes beyond mere practical cooperation in common projects (or its opposite, in conflict). It is only with other people that my own coping can make sense. They may or may not know what I am doing, and if they know, they may or may not agree with me. But it is only because my own actions and coping can make sense to *them* that they can make sense to *me*. To say that an action is refractory to making sense is a good start on calling it a failure (ἁμαρτία, disappointing, wrong, sin, and so on). The truly evil is usually at some level simply absurd, incapable of making sense.

To be a self is to cope in the world, as we have learned from Heidegger and his commentators. To be a self is to care for myself, something learned from others who first cared for me. To cope is to deal with opportunities and (when possible) fend off disappointments. In a word, we confront Exposure, Limitation, and Need, usually focused first on Limitation. We have to face mortality and get along with other people and their demands. Exposure and Need are more subtle, as often as not overlooked or invisible, but they lead to the things that matter most: self-definition and dependence on others.

So what do we do? We seek recognition for achievement, sometimes just recognition for being there. Acknowledge my presence! Recognition is judged by standards of a community of competents. Often recognition takes the form of money (payment for work), but that is only the most visible form of recognition. In a more crude form, we want to be the center of attention in order to get others to validate our own self-definition. That is largely a matter of narratives — my version, not my critics' version. This can be an attempt to get control, to evade Exposure, to cover up the problems in my own story, to deflect attention from troubled parts of it. Candor and honesty are also possible, of course, though people have privacy and personal boundaries in a narrative sense as well as other senses.

In effect, in the course of a life, a person grows into a narrative, hopefully a coherent one. So what gives a human life narrative coherence? That may not be so simple. In *Living in Spin*, we saw MacIntyre's reflections on Hamlet's problems, including his uncertainty about which kind of narrative he was living in. Sometimes we don't know what story we are part of (one more reason to pray the Kyrie). We have bumped into ambiguity again. We have ways of criticizing and of selecting between multiple narratives, but I don't know a systematic way we do that. Naturalistic ways of thinking offer many analogies, but that doesn't strike me as very helpful.

4.3 Ambiguity Again

Language brings ambiguity and only in language can one notice that language itself can give us things in the world in multiple ways. Likewise, only in language can one point out that stakes and interests are ambiguous. Having created ambiguity, language is also the medium for resolving it. Conflicts of interest are adjudicated in the social institutions of property[3] and social roles. Property and roles are necessary because stakes and the language that defines them are ambiguous and often in conflict. Along with property and roles go also rights, responsibilities, privileges, perquisites and all the other ways to regulate relations between persons. Society and life in society get much of their structure from the need to disambiguate the world. Look at some of the loci of ambiguity.

Ambiguity arises in the social construction of reality, basic life orientation, the structure of the world, however one takes the world to be. People disagree, and they care (and quarrel) about each other's versions of reality. It is in the logic of the concept of "reality" that it is not *just* a social construction in the sense of a work of art, caprice, whimsy or otherwise a matter of free choice. This — call it paradox or what you will — is the irony that Berger and Luckmann named in their title, *The Social Construction of Reality*. They named it, but it is a philosophical problem, and they scrupulously avoided philosophy in that book. Sociology was enough.

Restate the irony in regard to philosophy of religion. People disagree about starting points in shaping a basic orientation to the world, and it is logically impossible to argue *to* a starting point.[4] If one does, it is no longer the starting point. Starting is transferred to some other premises, possibly tacit, not spelled out, maybe not even recognized; in any case protected from criticism. The new starting point is nevertheless ample basis for an argument, especially if the structure of the logic is murky; then argument becomes both heated and intractable.

It is not as if people could just agree to disagree within some larger framework of an agreed-upon world. The larger framework is precisely what the disagreement is about. It is, of course, sometimes possible to agree to disagree in a social sense, and a society or culture can sometimes tolerate such disagreement and still survive, though doing that hides

---

[3] Both "things" (personal property) and territory (real property)

[4] Niebuhr, *Radical Monotheism*, 124 and *The Meaning of Revelation*, remarks on a confessional rather than apologetic method: first edition, p. viii, second edition, p. x, third edition, p. xxxiv. See also Porter, *Living in Spin*, 170.

a deep philosophical incoherence. How are we to acknowledge the social construction of our realities and yet still understand them *as* reality? Doing that will take some work.

Among the basic features of an orientation to the world are the choices between platonist realism, nominalism, and their alternatives; naturalisms and their alternatives; how to deal with the problem of formal causes; and how to handle the relation between individuals and society. We have already seen these issues.[5] Inasmuch as they are presuppositions, not conclusions, I simply assume without apology some answers. Naturalism is appropriate for the natural sciences, but much of the world lies beyond the sciences, where history and phenomenology, among other disciplines, make a kind of sense that the sciences cannot. In the choices about realism and nominalism the inquiry of this book lies in the tradition that passes through moderate realism and eventuates in modern hermeneutics.[6] The problem of formal causes may not be dismissed (as in materialisms); it has to be faced in the form "what is it about this thing that makes it be whatever it is?" The problem goes beyond what Aristotle and Aquinas have left us about formal causes. Unworkable kinds of individualism we have seen already. Together, these four, naturalism, nominalism, materialism, and individualism may go by the moniker "nanomind."[7] The nanomind ontology starts by privileging matter as the essence of being. In this study, matter*ing* is at least as important, for it is mattering that constitutes composite beings as whatever they are. The question, "which matter is part of such-and-such a being?" gets answered with "the things that matter." Mattering is human-relative — another source of radical ambiguity.

Along the way, one of the enduring controversies in Western philosophy is about determinism (and sometimes "free will"). It is sometimes alleged that physical motions are determined and so everything is determined, and on the tacit assumptions of such an inquiry, "there is no free will." To this it is fair to say that we do not live in a world of Laplacian determinism; not after quantum mechanics. We do not know what a Laplacian world would even be like, precisely because we do not live in such a world. That, however, is to deflect attention from the more radical point. Most "things" in the world are composite, and as just remarked above, what a thing is is constituted by the mattering that holds it together as *one*

---

[5] Porter, *The Accountant's Tale*, section 9.1.

[6] For an example of the differences, see Kenny, "Aquinas and Wittgenstein." He was not entirely happy with that article in hindsight, but it works as a starting point.

[7] Porter, *The Accountant's Tale*, section 9.1.

thing. Most "things" exist not in the set of elementary particles but in the power set of that set: the set of subsets of the set of elementary particles. It makes no difference what you take as elementary; the ontological role of mattering is the same. The power set is not just larger than the original set, by itself it doesn't determine which of its elements matter. Mattering is human-relative and so the being of things (and persons) in the world is human-relative, which takes it quite beyond questions about determinism or any other naturalistic considerations.

We come to the world in language and that can be done in many ways.[8] We somehow can criticize a text or artifact from another culture and place it in terms of our own worldview. How we do that is not always well understood. Suffice it to say that we can deal with the ambiguities that arise in the encounter of multiple conceptualities. We anticipate examples that will arise if we ever meet language-capable space aliens, so-called intelligent life from other planets around other stars. Our own being-in-the-world is shaped in so many contingent ways by the natural history of this planet and the evolutionary development of hominids and eventually of Homo sapiens and language. What about marine mammals, on our own planet? If anything is known in depth, it is known only in the technical literature. I don't think anyone has succeeded in talking to whales, or translating dolphin and whale songs. Not yet, but hopefully soon.

Language gives us a world of contingency, and where there is contingency and interests, there is narrative. This we have seen in section 3.3. All narratives are edited, which means that the author or editor has to decide what to include and what to leave out. What gets included has to be characterized, and what gets left out is obvious, uninteresting, just unknown, or embarrassing. An act gets its being from the narratives that can be told of it. This issue has arisen already for other people. In the relation between the Jesus story in the Gospels and the background in the Common Documents (the sacred texts shared in common by rabbinic Judaism and Christianity), there are parallels.[9] Edward Hobbs found five interpretations of this literary parallelism in other authors and then added three more of his own. The last, the eighth, anticipates what I have called the circular relation between narrative and action. Speaking of the Jesus events, Hobbs said,

---

[8] As Edward Hobbs argued in his treatment of conceptuality; see section 1.8 of *The Accountant's Tale*, "Understanding a Strange Culture."

[9] For some of them, see section 3.1 of *The Accountant's Tale*, "The Exodus in the Gospels."

> Unless the event of God which encounters us and calls us *does* come to language as divine event, it is not divine event, whatever else it is, and however beneficent it may otherwise be. The languaging of it is not an interpretation of the event-already-there, but the coming-to-be of the event; and if it is what the Christian tradition means by divine event, it will require languaging in terms of the models of that tradition.[10]

The ambiguity should be obvious: Why are *these* events (and this suffering) such a central act of God in history? Others could have been chosen, with different results for the character of ultimate reality. We shall see more in chapter 6 below.

Ambiguity of action has another root in addition to what we have seen. It arises in the evolution of animals, for it is with animals that motion initiated from within the organism is possible. Plants usually do not move; not in the sense that animals do. An animal moves, but where will it go next? That ambiguity has to be resolved, and the study of animal behavior as a discipline unto itself is devoted to answering that question. Action is possible only where there is ambiguity, because action resolves ambiguity. Contingency and interest are the basis for action. Ambiguity in action is one root or origin of the responsible liberty of interpretation that characterizes biblical religion. Exercise of that liberty was a major theme in *The Accountant's Tale*. Action is ambiguous not just in its "motions" (if any), but also in its ends and goals, what serves the interests of the actor. Interests are as open and ambiguous as the actions chosen to get to them. Interests shape a person. To structure (and sometimes restructure) them gives a life to the person.[11] If things go well, we can speak of "life more abundantly." In secular and non-partisan terms, that would mean "success" in life. In Christian biblical terms, success is usually called "salvation." It is what really living really is. Calling it salvation presupposes that it solves some characteristic problem of living, and in Christian terms that problem gets called "sin," but these terms require a careful re-understanding before they can make sense here.

Ambiguity underlies *analogy*. In view of the large role it has played in philosophical theology, analogy deserves more explanation than I know

---

[10] Hobbs, "Eight Interpretations."

[11] That would mean something like a "basic life orientation" or narrative coherence of a life, terms that I have never to my satisfaction explained. Like everything else here, they are ambiguous.

4.4 Responsibility

how to give it.[12] John Ellis remarked that in an analogy, we do not group like things together, but unlike things, in order that we may treat them in like ways. This, of course, was anticipated centuries ago at IV Lateran, which observed that in any analogy where some aspects of two things are similar, there are other aspects (and more of them) that are different. Suppose an analogy; why should we treat two things as similar when they are not? We deal with them in ways that are similar, but the similarity is similarity *for us*. To deal with things is to cope, and coping is the basic relation of human beings to the world. The being of things is in their mattering, so the being of things is in their relationship to human beings.[13] To say that the being of things that we can know is relative to human being could appear to open the way to a "fundamental ontology" or an "ontotheology," in Heidegger's words. On the contrary, this does not give us an ontotheology, for persons disagree and are in any case radically fallible. The purpose of ontotheology was to get control (as in many Christian platonisms) but we are not in control. What I am is incompletely determined; what I am is incompletely known or knowable; I have only a little control over who or what I am, but in the end I am not in control even of my own being. This is one reason why the experience of the sacred is also an experience of dread. The sacred is a clearing in which it is possible to see that I am at stake, at risk, and I am not in control. Above all, I am not in *conceptual* control. There is no ontotheology that can overcome this being-not-in-control (or resolve all ambiguities); ambiguity deflates any ontotheology and with it any Platonism. We are left with each other.

4.4 Responsibility

What do we do when we are up against irreducible ambiguity? Look again at Heidegger's definition of human being,[14] once its glaring mistake is corrected: Human being is the sort of being that matters to itself and to other beings like it; the mattering is ontological. It is not just *how* we be, it is *what* we are. In colloquial and somewhat sloppy language, persons are part of one another. More precisely, persons have stakes in each other and so persons have claims on other persons, just as other persons have claims on

---

[12] See Ellis on analogy also on pp. 57 and 101.
[13] Being-for-us is relative to us; being independent of us we cannot know. Cf. the ending of the *Tractatus*. To ask about being independent of us already specifies it relative to us.
[14] This, of course, is a midrash on the translator's version, not the original German.

me, in regard to whatever I am doing in coping with the world, in regard to my own being-in-the-world. If other persons have claims on me then I answer to them, and that is one definition of responsibility. Responsibility serves as the remedy for ambiguity because ambiguities have to be resolved by choice. Responsibility leads to transcendence, or, in another perspective, grace: living without platonist certainty, living without being in control. Even if we get control for a time and for limited circumstances, in the end, we are not in control.

Responsibility begins as a debt to particular others, to a community of responsibility, a community of competents, or in Richard Rubenstein's words, a community of moral obligation.[15] Rubenstein's definition was effectively a community in which members are responsible both *to* and *for* each other. The interests of one are shared by all; the majority may not expel a member on the premise that their interests do not include his interests.

All very fine, but *which* community are we speaking of? A person may be a member of many communities. In that observation, we can see that once again we are talking not about something simple that a preexisting person does but about a feature of the being of persons and personhood. Community membership is ambiguous. The issue first arose in the end of the constructive chapter in *Living in Spin* (§§5.4.3, 5.4.4). There are two issues pertinent here: whether membership is voluntary or not, and how we are to avoid taking community membership as the basis for tribal warfare. Membership is voluntary when the community is entered in a secondary socialization. These are communities by choice, communities one *joins*. They may be formal or informal. Membership is involuntary when membership in the community is unavoidable. These are communities that are intrinsic, one is a member because of what one is, not what one chooses. They begin with society itself, abstracting from particular societies, as in primary socialization, which is "the only game in town." While societies can be chosen or rejected (by immigration or emigration), not being a member of any society at all is not really an option. One always exists with respect to some society, even if one is an expatriate or in solitude. Societies may be voluntary but sociality is not. A society is not the only community one is a member of by virtue of what one is rather than by choice. There are many more; the community of language-capable

---

[15] Rubenstein, *After Auschwitz*, chapter 6, "Modernization and the Politics of Extermination."

4.4 Responsibility

life is one, and there is in some sense a "universal" community that one is a member of simply because of the structure of certain kinds of arguments in ethics or moral philosophy. More in a moment.

How are we to avoid tribal warfare? The answer, I think, is that we are members of many communities, some of them overlap, some are nested, and all are in some sense nested within the community of language-capable life.[16] If I am a Timson or a Malloy[17] it should be possible to find some reconciliation on the basis of interests and community membership larger than either clan.[18] Finding larger interests is not always easy.

So much for how community membership plays out in real life. This sort of conflict rests on ambiguity: which community membership is the one that "applies" in a situation before us? Ambiguity can arise in other ways as well, as when Antigone finds herself in the middle of conflicting moral obligations. But even there, obligations arise only in a community of some sort.

What is it that we want and can't get when we live in ambiguity? Disambiguation or resolution of all ambiguities? Do we want something that a platonism complete with ideal forms could give us? A platonism only appears to give us complete and certain answers; we never actually get them. It pretends to give us what we want, though what it gives us is hidden and invisible. Nevertheless, even hidden, it allays anxiety. We want a world that is exhaustively knowable and reliable, and it is the reliable part that really matters, although there is a lot of talk about a world that is knowable (but hidden from us). Instead, we settle for a world that answers some of our questions; more questions that we have not yet thought of can wait. Better answers will doubtless come, too, and they also can wait.

It is language that gives us a world, and language puts labels on things in the world. It underlies the skill of coping when it goes beyond labels and propositions, but that can be done in many ways. There are many languages, and within any language, there are many theories of how something works. (The example of phlogiston we have already seen.) We would like the security of *knowing* that the labels language gives us are *true* (and so reliable). In other words, we want to know that the world will support life more abundantly without raising issues of *troth* (interpersonation,

---

[16] There may be more beyond that, but I don't think we know much about it. Things may change after contact with space aliens, if that ever happens.

[17] Two clans of petty criminals in South London, in the world of Horace Rumpole.

[18] There are legends that something like that has happened with the Hatfields and the McCoys, real clans, and not fictional.

too risky), without too much challenge from other people. *Reliably* leads straight to troth and troth bumps into anxiety. We usually want out of anxiety. Anxiety is not just dread for my own risks and prospects, it is also dread of a kind of encounter with other people. They can know me, maybe better than I know myself; here, anxiety is fear of Exposure. It is also doubtless fear of conflict and opposition (Limitation). As for Need, there is more than demands on my time, effort, resources. I think the "more" is a demand on my caring for others, a demand on my efforts that is more primordial. It is a demand *that* I care. Care even when I can do nothing still costs me existentially. It changes who and what I am.

We have spoken of responsibility, other-relatedness and obligations, as the remedy for ambiguity. But how does responsibility work as a remedy? In the first place, we evidently have a responsible liberty of interpretation in coping with society and the world. I say "evidently" because it was newly recognized in the New Testament and in rabbinic claims that appeared later in the Talmuds. We have returned to the accountant who, when asked what is 2 × 2, answered with "what do you want it to be?" That kind of liberty can be frightening — or anxiety-conducive. In the story of the Oven of Achnai,[19] the problem in some ways goes unsolved and anxiety remains, though that is not pointed out.

The second way that a responsible liberty of interpretation operates is in hermeneutics, the practice of interpretation. What something is depends on the larger wholes that it is a part of. We have seen this in the case of the Resurrection texts, where *The Accountant's Tale* in section 8.1 found ten pertinent larger contexts and acknowledged that there may be many more. We can never know all the wholes: ambiguity remains. All interpretations are provisional. The hermeneutical circle is open to correction, and one way correction comes is in Exposure, Limitation, and Need, when some pain in life undermines the assumptions that we had brought to some problem. The pains are relative to our assumptions and inherited tradition, and so ambiguity remains even here.

What remains in this anxiety crisis, what won't go away? Ambiguity of course, but why? Ambiguity has many roots, but one is in the dual constitution of the Being of persons and things, in both matter and matter*ing*. Mattering cannot be objectivated in any naturalistic sense.[20] There

---

[19] My comments are in *The Accountant's Tale*, section 4.4.

[20] In the sense of Berger and Luckmann, others' massive subjectivity is a kind of objectivation, but it is a different kind.

4.4 Responsibility

is nothing one can point to about mattering that does not already presuppose mattering. Mattering contains an irreducible ambiguity, and at this point, we are up against transcendence, since nothing intramundane can resolve our questions. They are unanswerable.

We also face once again a question we have seen before and may again: how to speak responsibly to and of transcendence? Responsibility is no longer to real others in real communities but to an ideal Other and an ideal community beyond all others and communities. This is required in order to speak of "reality," real truth — but that contains an ambiguity which may be resolved: are we speaking of truth in some realist sense, or are we speaking of a kind of *troth* that we attribute to ultimate reality? Otherwise, there is just caprice and whimsy; language fails to grasp world, as in George Steiner's diagnosis of our own time above. Then all is illusion as in some South Asian religions, where the world is *mara* or *maya*.[21]

One problem along the way is that we naturally speak of an ideal Other and an ideal community of responsibility. But it does not follow from nominalizing them that we have to reify or objectivate them. In this sense we are following exemplars such as pseudo-Dionysius and John of Damascus rather than, say, John Duns Scotus. We shall return to Damascene's treatment below, at p. 95.

---

[21] See for example Westphal, *God, Guilt, and Death*, 31 and chapter 9.

Chapter 5

The Fate of Transcendence

In chapter 2 we sketched the way from language and world to an encounter with other people, at the threshold of transcendence. Yet many ask whether transcendence can still make sense in our culture, the culture of the West as it appears in America. (Europe may speak for itself.) Some traditional language games about God are certainly still played and played by many Americans. And indeed, in Africa, Christianity in some traditional sense is thriving and growing. Yet there has been a trend toward "secularization," one of the features of which is simply to dispense with any explicit transcendence. Some colloquial phrases survive without theory or structure or explanation.[1] To handle transcendence that way would be to do so without much recognition or intention, and it would all but inevitably leave out the historical commitments of biblical religion, without which it wouldn't really be biblical religion.

Sociologists have not come to an explanation for secularization, and I think that is because they are not (speaking as sociologists) able to ask questions that are essentially philosophical or theological. All they can offer is correlations between social phenomena, and interesting as they are, they don't really answer questions in philosophy or theology. The questions they ask in survey research are nevertheless not innocent of philosophy and theology, despite the efforts of sociology to bracket such questions. They can quote the people they survey, but they import thereby the assumptions of those they survey. We have to do better.

So we continue from the results in the previous chapters, on ambiguity

---

[1] As in Porter, *Basic Concepts*, 90 and section 6.5, where a few examples from colloquial and secular language are explored.

and interpersonhood and language. Transcendence has become interesting again, in the sense of being no longer obvious. The primary naiveté we all grew up with is available, but it cannot be continued *naively* once we encounter the challenges of critical thinking that are implicit in the world of our culture. We are in quest of secondary naiveté.[2] Primary naiveté is not really welcome in philosophical thinking, though philosophers can be amazingly naive nonetheless. It is still available in art and literature, where it travels with irony, and the results can be quite challenging.

5.1 Irony in Narrative

Our theme is living in the ambiguity of language. In one form, that is irony: a narrative with multiple meanings, one in which the characters do not entirely understand the narrative(s) they are acting in. Two movies will provide some lessons: *Empire of the Sun*[3] and *Lord of the Flies*.[4] Both movies, made from books, tell us things beyond what the original novels said, and they tell us in a way beyond what the original novels could. We are dealing with revisions, or "re-visioning," and in them we have examples of ambiguity in narrative. In addition, they both show us aspects of their action that the characters themselves do not and cannot know. Authors frequently tell us things that their characters do not know, but seldom does that ignorance become so thematic as in these two movies.

First, *Empire of the Sun*. The novel was based on the author's own experiences, though it was fiction. (The experiences in his autobiography were noticeably different.) In the novel, Jamie Graham as a boy lived in Shanghai with his parents in the late 1930s. He became separated from them as the war began and spent the next four years or so in an internment camp near Shanghai. The book has many atrocities, dead faces covered with flies. It is told in a somewhat matter-of-fact way, without editorializing or implications for life. American movie-goers would not stomach dead faces covered with flies, so something had to be done on the way to a movie version.

---

[2] The distinctions are Paul Ricoeur's, in the end of *The Symbolism of Evil*. We bumped into them as they appear in the Resurrection in Chapter 8 of *The Accountant's Tale*,

[3] It was based on a novel of the same name by James G. Ballard. The movie starred Christian Bale and was directed by Steven Spielberg.

[4] The novel was by William Golding, and the movie was made by Peter Brook.

Tom Stoppard (writing) and Steven Spielberg (directing) have given the story a coherence it did not have in the book, which was somewhat episodic. The singing and the music in the soundtrack bind together all that follows. They provide the function of a chorus, interpreting the action for the viewers in a way that is dubiously possible in a novel. The movie opens with Jamie, a boy soprano in the Anglican cathedral choir in Shanghai, singing a Welsh lullaby, Suo Gan, in Welsh. He is distracted and not entirely paying attention. Here is one verse in English:

> Sleep child on my bosom
> Cozy and warm is this;
> Mother's arms are tight around you,
> Mother's love is under my breast;
> Nothing may affect your napping,
> No man will cross you;
> Sleep quietly, dear child,
> Sleep sweetly on your mother's breast.[5]

Suo Gan tells a child that all's right with the world, the child is safe, it can sleep in peace.

> Harm will not meet you in sleep,
> Hurt will always pass you by.[6]

And for Jamie, that is almost true, though he is deeply scathed by what happens to him and around him.

As Peter Berger said in *A Rumor of Angels*, that everything is alright is one of the more outrageous claims about life and the world, even if it is sometimes true for a few days in the life of a protected child. The message is reinforced in the soundtrack, which includes a motet on the first lines of Psalm 33: Exsultate justi Domino — Rejoice in the Lord, O you Righteous. This is a slightly daring commentary on Europeans in an internment camp in Shanghai in World War II. It was a world of death, depredation, starvation, failure of the ordinary human supports of civilization. Exsultate justi is entirely gratuitous, not part of the story at all — in effect the commentary of a chorus. It is, I suppose, justifiable in the world of the story

---

[5] The translation is from the Wiki article, accessed 2015-10-22.

[6] The words are from the "looser rhythmic" translation in the Wiki article on Suo Gan. The echoes of Psalm 91, Night Prayer for Sundays, should not be missed. The ironies should be obvious, and Peter Berger remarked them in *Rumor of Angels*.

simply because the good guys win in the end, Jamie Graham survives and is reunited with his parents — but that ending could be read in the light of the ending of Job.

The irony should be clear enough. We never learn whether Jamie Graham knows the meaning of the words he sings. Nothing in the movie suggests that he does. If that is so, then the main character does not know what is happening in his life, his actions, or in the world around him, extend it as far as you like, all the way out, all the way to ultimate reality. His unknowing is highlighted when, near the end, after Basie (an American adult who took Jamie under his care) has killed the Japanese boy who saved Jamie's life earlier, Jamie tries CPR to resuscitate him, with the words, "I can bring anybody back," as he had done earlier in the hospital.[7] Again, Jamie more than once himself comments on the action in the words of the paradigm of the first conjugation of Latin verbs, "amo, amas, amat; amatus sum, amatus es, amatus est." The *meaning* of the paradigm is normally of no interest, and clearly he does not really understand the irony in what he is saying.

Narratives do many things and one of them, for this narrative, is affirmation of life in this world as good — in full view of all its pains. The precariousness of such an affirmation is one of the main points of *Empire of the Sun*. To point out that the affirmation of life in this world is also one of the most basic features of biblical religion is almost pedantic but perhaps necessary. Not everybody agrees with that affirmation. To make that affirmation is always to be in a state of at least partial ignorance about life and the world, for we never entirely know what we are doing.

Look at what biblical religion supposedly is: the affirmation that life in this world, as created, is good. That affirmation is made in full view of the manifold pains and evils of life. More than once later in the movie, Jamie (or Jim, as he has become) sings Suo Gan again. As a trio of Japanese kamikaze fighters prepare to take off, he sings in admiration for them. We never find out whether he knows Welsh or not, which is fitting: neither he nor we know what we are doing when we promise to affirm human life in this world as good, in full view of its pains. We are destroyed by those pains. Only knowing that can we *honestly* affirm life in this world as good. The scene is more than a little bit ironic. Does Jamie know these are kamikaze pilots? We never find out. Maybe. He just salutes

---

[7] A little after 2h 15m in the DVD. At 2h 17m 35s, as Jim is doing CPR on his Japanese friend, the body turns into Jim himself. What does that say?

them with his singing. As the kamikazes are airborne, American fighters attack, and Jamie rejoices, "P-51 Mustang! Cadillac of the skies!" Dr. Rawlins comes up to the roof Jamie is standing exposed on and tries to get him to come down. Jamie is so excited and out of control that Dr. Rawlins has to embrace him to get him to calm down. Jamie almost cries, in a complete change of attunement, "I can't remember what my parents look like." Then, in Dr. Rawlins' embrace, he begins the paradigm in the passive: "amatus sum, amatus es, amatus est." Let the reader sort out the ironies; there are more than these in the dialogue, not the least of which is Dr. Rawlins to Jamie, "Try not to think so much."

Now look at *Lord of the Flies*. Boys from a boarding school in England are thrust onto a tropical island separated from civilization, and things soon turn bad. The story is simple enough: a few dozen boys are flown out of England for safety during a major war, possibly nuclear, though we don't see that. Alone without adult supervision on an island off Australia, they degenerate into savages rather quickly. Two die and the rest are trying to kill a third when the Royal Navy arrives and saves them from themselves.

The movie is marked by several occurrences of the Kyrie Eleison, some not very obvious. In the beginning (1m 25s), at the boarding school, there is a brief still of the choir, singing the Kyrie, but to a fairly classical musical setting. Once noticed, it is a striking similarity between the two movies. They both begin with a boys' choir. In *Flies*, they sing the Kyrie Eleison (1m 8s to 1m 42s). In *Empire of the Sun*, they sing "Suo Gan." In neither do they really understand what they are singing.

The opening Kyrie is easy to miss, for the opening is just soundtrack and a slide-show, on the way to the evacuation and plane crash that deposits the boys alone on an unnamed island. At 3m 35s, there is a map of the Pacific, so the plane taking the boys away from the war is plausibly headed for Australia. A few of the boys find each other and begin to talk about what to do, when the choir comes marching down the beach, each boy with a black medieval biretta and cape with a cross insignia on the left breast, like Crusader knights (9m 35s). Again they sing the Kyrie, but to a different musical setting — one very modernistic and somewhat dissonant — and somewhat military, a marching song. In what follows, the choir supplies the worst actors, though their actions affect all the rest. At 1h 0m 12s ff., the Kyrie is sung by the choir again, as they disappear into the jungle. They are followed by one boy looking at the pig's head on a stake, attracting flies. In the end, they are rescued by officers and men of

5.1 Irony in Narrative

HMS Troubridge. The Kyrie returns as soundtrack at the end of the movie, during the credits.

In the movie, the boys do not know the meaning of the Kyrie. Sometimes they cannot even hear it. We can, as it is just soundtrack. But their actions are nevertheless transformed by it, and that is part of the puzzles of the distributed ontology of human action.[8] For us, the lesson: we do not know what we have done, but we know quite enough to be guilty. The Joke is on us.

Empire of the Sun was sunny and upbeat by comparison with *Lord of the Flies*. Not only do we not know what we are promising when we undertake our baptismal vows, we don't know what we ourselves bring to them. Baptism originally meant the foundering of a ship, shipwreck, or in the words of H. Richard Niebuhr, the failure of all our causes. But what if we ourselves are at fault? What if we don't understand our own roles in the story? *Lord of the Flies* gives us that. The Royal Navy brings a larger context in which the boys' savagery can be relativized — and presumably redeemed, though we don't see that. Again, as in the short ending of Job, the problems of the story go unsolved, though *Lord of the Flies* is candid about that — in the ending of Job that we have, unanswerable questions get raped by the pious. To put it a little differently, the movie resists reduction to the theories one finds in dogmatic theology, about human nature and human sin. We are in the land of irony, not of propositions. The movie has been taken as a depiction of original sin.[9]

Empire of the Sun, like *Lord of the Flies*, gives us features that were not in the book. Stoppard and Spielberg have done more than just interpreting the action for us, as a chorus would. They show us that the actors do not understand their own world. They do not hear what we hear, and they do not know what it tells us. In this sense, they do not understand either themselves or their own world.

Irony in narrative cries for transcendence. In both movies, the problem is cut off artificially when the protagonists are rescued: In *Lord of the Flies*, by the Royal Navy; in *Empire of the Sun*, by the Allied victory and liberation of the internment camps. In effect, the narratives here confess that the problem cannot be solved in any way that would allow or license a

---

[8] See Porter, *Living in Spin*, especially chapter 5.

[9] Its radical and insidious depravity is more than I could address in chapter 7 of *Living in Spin*, which considered the phenomenon only for limited and restricted purposes. For a more pointed exploration of original sin, see Golding's novel *Darkness Visible*.

rationalistic solution. The irony is unbearable, and we cry for relief. Thus do the stories respect unanswerable questions, but they can be interpreted as *answering* unanswerable questions — another instance of the Joke with which we began this book. If ultimate reality implies our creaturehood, not being in control, then unanswerable questions and irony in narrative will show themselves. They are not susceptible of proof. Any choice of ultimate reality is circular, because to speak of reality always already presupposes some knowledge of reality.[10]

5.2 Objectivation

Ambiguity led us to irony in literature, but philosophical theology tries to get out of both ambiguity and irony. They are too painful. Look at the principle ways to escape from them. Most of them involve objectivation, usually objectivation of God and of transcendence. Objectivation solves many problems, usually by appearing to answer unanswerable questions. The two movies leave unanswerable questions unanswered. Objectivation would provide answers to the question implicit in both movies: How do we deal with what we do not know about ourselves, our actions, our place in the larger world? Thereby objectivation relieves anxiety and resolves ambiguity. It hides the questions it does not answer.

Objectivation is not the only way to mishandle a relationship to transcendence but it is one of the more common ways. The examples of objectivation are not very systematic: Visible images, proofs and argumentative apologetics, Humean "miracles," an anthropomorphic deity, a literalist Resurrection, literalism more generally, sacred canopies, and subverting analogy into univocation are all examples. The original instance of objectivation was visible images of the gods, including the one God, prohibited in the Common Documents. There are places where objectivation is appropriate, as in the naturalism of classical physics, but that is not what the present inquiry asks about. We are trying to make sense of human life in the world as a whole, which includes a lot more than what the sciences can illuminate.

The word *ob-ject* is a compound that means to throw out (*jacio*) in front (*ob*): in other words, put something out in front of everybody so people can see it. In effect, that hides the interpretive acts by which humans

---

[10] Cf. Porter, *Unwelcome Good News*, chapter 4, and *Basic Concepts*, section 5.6, "Hermeneutical Circularity."

5.2 Objectivation

can know some thing or phenomenon (including other persons) in order to concentrate on whatever it is apart from human interpretation. It's a way of saying, just accept the interpretation; allow us to build on it by tacitly presupposing it — which hides it.

Objectivation often happens in a logical transformation wherein some phenomenon starts with a linguistic nominalization, which is to say a noun is created to deal with it. From nominalization, the logic proceeds to reify the phenomenon as a thing, by a hypostatization that consummates the objectivation of it. In the natural sciences, this is a necessary move in order to examine the world and things in it "sub specie naturae," under the aspect of nature. It is also an essential part of a systems ontology, which is presupposed by the sciences.[11] In dealing with other persons and with transcendence, objectivation is not a good move, for it hides what is of most interest and protects objectivators from exposure to the other persons (or to God). Objectivation is a pathological form of interpersonation, for it treats persons as tools or things. I think people generally know this, and know both how to do it to other people and also how to defend themselves against other people who would do it to them.

Objectivation defends against certain kinds of challenge from other people. The other knows me, maybe better than I know myself. The other knows "into" my privacy, gets inside of my personal boundaries. Is objectivation of another's body ever appropriate? Not if sex is an issue; perhaps, if one is a surgeon, though surgeons operate in a larger background which is not objectivating at all. Can objectivation suspend interpersonation? It can bracket the personal, perhaps. But suspend the personal? What would that mean? I always interpersonate when I deal with something, even when I objectivate it, because its reality-for-me is shared with other people. I interpersonate toward them — always — even if I do not interpersonate *toward* the thing before us in the world. This is not a theory of panpsychism. That we meet other persons when we deal with spoons does not mean that spoons are personal beings. They are just tools, zuhanden.

Consider at least three senses of objectivation. In the first, from the sociology of knowledge, objective reality is what other people tell me it is. The massive intersubjectivity of everybody around me is very difficult to argue with.[12] If the people around me disagree among themselves,

---

[11] Porter, *Living in Spin*, chapter 3, especially sections 3.1 and 3.3.4.
[12] See Berger and Luckmann, *The Social Construction of Reality*, for the exposition of how some reality is first externalized, then objectivated, then internalized by newcomers.

then objectivation in this sense crumbles. We began above with the second meaning of objectivation, the semantic transformation in which a nominalization becomes reification and then hypostatization or objectivation. The third meaning of objectivation has been with us everywhere, hiding the human origins of socially constructed realities, usually in bad faith.

Of these features of objectivation, the one most interesting is the last, evasion. It is a way of closing oneself off to another who would know me when I don't want to be known. Thereby, it is a way of getting control over the relationship to the other person. This is not just about intramundane other people, it is about transcendence, when we interpersonate beyond all other people. The risk is not just unwelcome being-known but also being alone, abandoned. That people want to evade such a personal encounter attests their fear of a real personal encounter with transcendence.

5.3 Visible Images

It all started with visible images (idols) in the ancient world. The biblical sources were not capable of modern philosophy about objectivation, but their instinct was to avoid visible images, molten statues especially. A statue is the paradigm of putting the concept "out there" where people can see it. It embodies all the features of a nature religion, from which the new religion of history was radically different. The gods of nature religions were characteristically different. But biblical religion emerged by slow stages from nature religion, and idols were present until the Exile, maybe later. (Idols were common outside biblical religion well into the Common Era.) What is not obvious without close reading is that the prohibition applied equally to images of the one God, HaShem himself. The texts are not particularly systematic. Exodus 20.4–6 (E) applies to images of anything and implies the worship of them. The golden calf appears in Exodus 32.1b–4 (E), but in 32.5 (J), the calf is the one God who brought the Israelites out of Egypt. Reproaches follow (32.7–14, D; 32.15–20, J, and 32.21–24, E). In 1 Kings 12.28–29, Jeroboam sets up the two golden calves at Dan and Bethel, an offense revolting to the nose of the Deuteronomistic Historian for the duration of the Northern Kingdom, and probably the reason for tracing the memory back to the Exodus itself. But the texts are at least open to the interpretation that the images are of the one God who brought them out of Egypt, not necessarily images of other gods.

See also section 2.2 above.

5.3 Visible Images

The Deuteronomist and the Yahwist have noticeably different attitudes toward idols. The Deuteronomist is outraged. The JE texts satirize idols: when Rachel steals her father Laban's household idols, Laban comes after them and they have to hide in a port-a-potty (Genesis 31.35, E). We see by stages the emergence of historical monotheism from polytheistic nature religion.

In the Common Era theologians have not agreed on the extent of the prohibition: whether to any living thing, to the saints, or just to God the Father. My Church bends the rules for itself and its art. A trick question for you: How many commandments are there in the Ten Commandments? Answer: at least eleven, which is typical of the Bible. If it says n and you can actually count, you will often find $n + 1$. This is why Protestants and Catholics can number the commandments differently; you have to combine two to come out with ten and not eleven.

In the Catechism, the second commandment (Protestant numbering), about visible images, is in Catholic numbering lumped in with the first (no other gods), on the not very explicit presupposition that images could only be of other gods. Michelangelo and the ceiling of the Sistine Chapel is the obvious case of a visible image of God the Father. Statues are rare, if there are any at all. But Michelangelo is not the only exception to the rule. It is possible to weasel out of the meaning of the biblical texts, but to do so hides and evades the reason why hearing and texts are permitted but seeing and visible images are not. It is not just abuse by visual representation that the text warns against. Abuse of language is also possible: it follows in the next commandment, on taking the Name of God in vain. That idea gets repeated in the Lord's prayer, in the "may your name be holy."

In the Common Era, objectivation has been more subtle and insidious. It is rarely candid, but it happens when we reason about God with the same logic we use for objects. The first millennium didn't do too badly but the second, since the high Middle Ages, has not done as well. Its habit of reasoning about transcendence in propositions more appropriate to the intramundane has come down to us in Analytic philosophy of religion.

5.4 Proofs

We have seen the trouble with proofs already in *The Accountant's Tale*.[13] The point here is merely to observe that they are a form of objectivation. In *The Accountant's Tale*, we saw that alleged proofs of the so-called "existence" of God or the validity of Christianity[14] are all faulty in one way or another. Classic rebuttals to particular proofs can be left to the literature, where they abound. My own central objection here is that any such proof is an attempt to prove a starting point and trying to prove a starting point is always viciously circular. Starting points are presupposed and chosen, not proven. The function of proofs is quite different from what is alleged of them. They allay anxiety, and they hide the role of believers in choosing their own basic life orientation. That is bad faith.

In *The Accountant's Tale*, we followed the career of "miracles" along with the distinctions in the Definition of Chalcedon for several reasons. The concept of miracle was replaced by that of a clearing, a place in life where it is possible to see reality as it really is, a place where ultimate reality shows itself. A clearing is ambiguous, especially in a culture without the modern scientific faith in the reliability and consistency of nature. If the proposed ultimate reality is biblical, a clearing takes on the character of a challenge or invitation to faith. Yet it can also be mistaken for a "proof" of the correctness of faith. To treat it as a proof is to objectivate the meaning of the clearing, to misrepresent choice as necessity (an act of bad faith). This is a form of irresponsibility, for it hides or denies the role of human interpreters in the understanding of whatever it is that we are trying to understand. People don't agree about ultimate reality. More importantly, we are up against the limits of language, where language's reach exceeds its grasp, where we cannot comprehend. As always, we would like to understand a little about our not-understanding: how it arises, how to make sense of it responsibly.

Proof objectivates. It is in the nature of proofs that they reason with propositions, and propositions throw out before an audience whatever it is they are about. Yet we begin by talking *to* God and then move to talking *about* God, but not necessarily as philosophers do. Consider the Psalms, which are full of talk both to and about God, but they do not do philosophical theology, and in the Psalms, proof would be unthinkable. If one

---

[13] See *The Accountant's Tale*, sec. 5.2, "Proofs of God," and sec. 7.6 "The pathologies of proofs."

[14] The rabbis have more sense than to attempt proof.

5.4 Proofs

looks at the acts of God sought or celebrated in the Psalter, their variety is bewildering — if one wants theoretical coherence or order. They arise in the course of events and in the minds and mouths and lives of suppliants.

Consider a few landmarks in the history of proofs in philosophical theology. The Oath Against Modernism, that the so-called "existence" of God can be proven by reason unaided by faith, begins thus:

> And first of all, I profess that God, the origin and end of all things, can be known with certainty by the natural light of reason from the created world (see Rom. 1:19), that is, from the visible works of creation, as a cause from its effects, and that, therefore, his existence can also be demonstrated:

> Secondly, I accept and acknowledge the external proofs of revelation, that is, divine acts and especially miracles and prophecies as the surest signs of the divine origin of the Christian religion and I hold that these same proofs are well adapted to the understanding of all eras and all men, even of this time.[15]

First reason and then "miracles" provided Vatican I with objectivation of God. Reason takes the form of proofs, sometimes explanations mistaken for proofs.

There have been many alleged proofs. They have problems, as some examples may illustrate. One that gets most of the attention is in Aquinas's *Summa Theologica* 1.2.3, and since it has five parts, it goes by the name the "Five Ways" of proving the existence of God. It is not original with Aquinas, though Aquinas has cleaned it up and made it more orderly and systematic than the source from which he got it. That source is in John of Damascus, in *The Exposition of the Orthodox Faith*, whom we mentioned on p. 83 only to defer his remarks to this point.

The *Exposition of the Orthodox Faith* begins with some of the same issues that Aquinas later does in the *Summa*; among them proving[16] the "existence" of God and other preliminary matters. Aquinas follows the structure of Damascene's logic.

---

[15] Quoted from the source at http://www.papalencyclicals.net/Pius10/p10moath.htm.

[16] But David Burrell someplace observes that Aquinas does not use the usual verb for prove (*demonstrare*), but rather *probare*, which may have a subtly different meaning.

I put "existence" in scare-quotes for a reason, and it is a reason that Damascene explains, if one reads him carefully. For Damascene, God is beyond being and so I presume is not *a* being.

> For He does not belong to the class of existing things: not that He has no existence, but that He is above all existing things, nay even above existence itself.[17]

The Greek text attracts anachronisms from moderns who would like to help its meaning along.

> Οὐδὲν γὰρ τῶν ὄντων ἐστίν· οὐχ ὡς μὴ ὤν, ἀλλ᾽ ὡς ὑπὲρ πάντα τὰ ὄντα, καὶ ὑπὲρ αὐτὸ τὸ εἶναι ὤν.[18]

This is pretty simple Greek and the translation above is justifiable, though the translator has made some choices that bear remark. Greek has two words for negation, οὐχ and μή. Of the two, the second is by far the stronger, where the first leaves room for nuance, and John takes advantage of that distinction in order to make his point. In effect, he says that God is not a being. There is no Greek word behind the translator's "class" of existing beings. And that raises the issue that the translator has to decide but does not force how it is to be decided. Greek has only the verb 'to be,' εἶναι and its forms. I am not aware of a Greek verb for the modern concept 'exist,' and although Latin has *existere*, it is late and originally meant stand out rather than exist. Any translator's rendering is not innocent of philosophical choices. One might say that for John of Damascus it is a category error to think of God as "a" being, and so of God as "existing," something that only beings can do.

Speaking in my own words and not Damascene's, God does many things, but existing is not one of them.[19] Or, if you like, there is a God, but he does not exist. That can be said in English but not in Damascene's Greek. God *causes* to exist beings that do exist, and that is one thing that makes them *created*. That, of course, is a highly ironic use of the term 'cause,' for far from providing an intramundane cause or explanation, it marks in language a place where questions have no answers.[20] One could

---

[17] John of Damascus, *Exposition of the Orthodox Faith*, 10. See Part I, chapter 4, in the penultimate paragraph.

[18] Migne, PG, vol. 94, col. 800. On the Net at http://patristica.net/graeca (Accessed 2019-06-18).

[19] As we saw already on p. 39.

[20] Cf. p. 40, the term 'God' is a place in language where we deal with unanswerable questions, though not by answering them.

call the irony of this language a deliberate category error. Some can hear that irony, some who can hear will not. Some are in revolt against it, some celebrate in it. Those who can hear the irony and entrust their lives to it exult in it. Once again, we are at a place where our theological guides have done their best to mark a reality that is not capable of being objectivated, but people objectivate it anyway.

Aquinas's Five Ways are widely taken to prove the "existence" of the God of biblical religion, thus objectivating at least part of what (or whom) the believer believes in. Closer examination turns up problems with any such easy reading of them. Recent Thomists have argued that the Five Ways do not prove very much,[21] if they were even intended as proofs; the unicity of God comes later, and identification with the God of the Bible later still, and the last only by faith. Thomas says as much in the *Summa Theologica* 1.1.8, when he asks, "Whether sacred doctrine is a matter of argument?" and answers in the negative. Some faith is required. Nevertheless, there is something right in the Five Ways, even if it is not very clear. They argue that there is something like ultimate reality, though they don't say much about what it is. The conclusion of each of the Five Ways, the "quod omnes dicunt deum" and words like it, is a gratuitous assertion without either explanation or argument. Thomas has moved too fast. On the other hand, if the arguments are construed as to an unspecified ultimate reality, they are one way of explaining how things start. In another, if we bracket Paul Tillich's Liberal theology, he nevertheless deserves credit for observing that we all have some concept of ultimate reality ("u-r," sometimes abbreviated in these pages), whether or not we articulate it or spell it out. Most of the time, we don't. For Tillich, it is something like "ultimate concern," a phrasing somewhat different from Aquinas's.

There is another classic question that should be handled in the same way, the existence of the world outside our senses. It became an issue in the seventeenth century but it was known long before. Aristotle (in the *Physics* II.2 193a2-8) remarks that the existence of nature (i.e., the world) is so obvious that it would be counterproductive to attempt to prove it. On the contrary, Kant opined, the great philosophical scandal of his time was the lack of proof of the existence of the "external" world. Heidegger followed Aristotle: he laughed — the scandal was not the failure of proof but the very attempt to prove something so obvious, a necessary presupposition of

---

[21] O'Callaghan, "Can We Demonstrate that 'God Exists'?"

all reasoning.

That there "is" some sort of ultimate reality is obvious. That people disagree about what it is is also obvious. It takes a lot of work to get from mere ultimate reality to the God of historical-covenantal religion, as indeed, it does in Aquinas. It is a long way from the "Deus" in "quod omnes dicunt deum" in the Five Ways to the God of the Bible. The meaning changes along the way.

A similar change of meaning appears in each of the Five Ways, when to ask "why?" silently moves from seeking intramundane causes to asking for something "divine." Thomas does not call it transcendence, for he does not to my knowledge distinguish the intramundane from the transcendent in the way the modern world does. The change in meaning on the way from intramundane causes to "quod omnes dicunt Deum" is subtle and easily missed. The language is ambiguous. In asking "why?," does it seek some explanation like the causes already found in the world, or does the inquirer ask (and know he asks) *after* explanations have done all they can?[22]

The alternative to D. Z. Phillips is a kind of rationalism that reasons about transcendence in the same way we reason about intramundane things. It begins not as a thesis, nor a set of spelled-out axioms, but as a method. The method is enforced simply in demands that the sparring partner supply reasons and justifications in order to qualify as responsible. Yet in that method there lie implicit substantive claims. This rationalism presupposes in its method that the things it reasons about (e.g., God) can be reasoned about as it does — in the same way it reasons about, say, the "God particle," sometimes known as the Higgs boson. The purpose of this rationalism is to get control over the things it reasons about — at least conceptual control. And that makes it a very poor method for thinking about our own *not* being in control, our own creaturehood.

"Irrationalism" is a rationalist term of obloquy. It is also very misleading, insinuating that the alternative to rationalism is irrationalism. On the contrary, the alternative to rationalism is *not* irrationalism but rather a kind of caution and circumspection in thinking. All too often, philosophers rush in where even fools fear to tread. Akin to "irrationalism" is the word "fideism," another term of endearment coined by rationalists to stigmatize their adversaries as wrong without actually having to make a case

---

[22] Phillips, *The Problem of Evil*, 133–134. It is cited and quoted at length in Porter, *Basic Concepts of Biblical Religion*, 82, in chapter 6.

against them. What rationalists (or propositionalists, equally) accuse their adversaries of is *irresponsibility*. The irresponsible fail to discharge some obligation that is incumbent on them. But people do not agree on what the responsibilities of faithful theologians and philosophers are. They don't agree on starting premises for logical argument by reason. They don't even agree on how language engages transcendence — whether adequately in propositions, or whether the capacities of language beyond propositions are needed to enable transcendence to show itself. What is more, responsibility is always responsibility *to* some community of competents, whether real or ideal.[23]

5.5 Analogy

Traditionally, the doctrine of analogy comes from scholastic philosophy, though at least some parts of it go back to Aristotle, who knew the concept. The four best-known kinds of analogy are given by Cajetan in commentary on Aquinas, whom Gregory Rocca quotes: "There are, then, four kinds of analogy: inequality, attribution, metaphorical proportionality, and proper proportionality, although only the last is genuine analogy..."[24] Cajetan has usually spoken for the scholastic tradition until recent disputes. Some would like to use analogy in its scholastic form today. We are fortunate to have maintenance and technical support from Thomists, but I think the problem needs to be re-understood from the bottom up, which is more than I can do. We need to do for our own problems and our own time what Thomas did for his time, learning from him where we can and accounting for differences of context when we must.

We can learn a lot from the history of the concept of analogy and the controversies surrounding it. It is one choice among at least two others — treating religious language as univocal or treating it as equivocal simply. And even that does not exhaust the traditional possibilities; for some treat analogy as a third kind of discourse, others treat it as a kind of equivocation. My starting point was David Burrell, *Knowing the Unknowable God*, p. 17. Treating religious language as univocal courts great hazards. He names two and others have named more. Univocation tends either to deprecate the world before God in pathological ways or to draw God into

---

[23] See *Living in Spin*, section 5.4.4, "Responsibility in Community and Narrative."

[24] Rocca gives an extended exposition of analogy in Aquinas with its principal textual sources in chapter 5 of *Speaking the Unknowable God*, especially p. 114.

the world on the world's terms. He didn't deal with the insidious tendency of univocal language to hide the fact that human religious language is a human social construction, for which humans are responsible.[25] Human choice is candidly acknowledged in Joshua 24 and in Mark 8.27–30 and parallels.

These hazards can be spelled out so that readers can avoid them but that doesn't always work very well. In practice, analogical language is easily subverted so that believers can enjoy the comforts and illusions of univocal language without facing the anxiety that comes with candor about analogical language. Pastors are reluctant to disturb or challenge people they think are simple believers. The tradition continues, and then degenerates into learned superstition.

Begin again, trying to understand our own problematic. In at least some parts of the tradition, Being is taken as an act and God as the actor. Sometimes this is traced back to Exodus 3.14, God's answer to Moses, translated as "I am who [I] am," or the like. This is taken as a license for Greek philosophy of Being, and as far as it goes, that may not be a bad thing. I would prefer another translation — or paraphrase, John Courtney Murray's. God answers Moses' question, "Who are you?" with "I shall be with you as who I am shall I be with you."[26] The Platonic-Aristotelian problem of 'Being,' whatever that means, is deferred to some other day. The Hebrew, *eyeh asher eyeh*, is about interpersonal faithfulness. Moses has asked whether the God will be *with* him. The answer is yes, but not on Moses's terms. This is the issue in acts of God: the *presence* of God, the *mitsein* of God, in Heidegger's very incomplete terms. If God acts, then we are not alone; if God does not act, then we are alone. If we can say that ultimate reality acts, then it plays the role of the void that begins as an enemy, then is indifferent, and in the end becomes a companion.[27]

This grows from a less traditional way of treating Being as an act. The question of acts of God arose in the distributed ontology (*Living in Spin*, sec. 5.3.2), but it appeared only in passing, in a book preoccupied with human action. In *Spin*, an act was defined to occur in a situation that combines contingency and interest, narrated in such a way that the contingency is the effect of an actor. In the central prototype case (human

---

[25] See section 2.2 and the works discussed there.

[26] Murray, *The Problem of God*, 10. See also *The Accountant's Tale*, section 2.3, "The Name," especially the citations to Westphal and his further citations.

[27] A paraphrase of Niebuhr in *Radical Monotheism*, 123–124, where he quotes Alfred North Whitehead.

5.5 Analogy

action), the act is narratable by the actor in the narrative. In the case of acts of God, this is no longer so. The divine actor does not narrate his own acts; not in any literal sense.[28]

We are indeed living in analogical language. Rather than follow the classical explanations of the kinds of analogy, I would like to start with a point made by John Ellis about misunderstanding language. Above, in section 3.1, p. 57, we heard Ellis say that "verbal categories group *unlike* things" together. It is a common assumption that when we say there is an analogy between two things, it is because there is some likeness between them. Ellis protests that the likeness is not in what they *are* but rather in how we *treat* them. Maybe I should put the emphasis a little differently: the likeness is in how *we* treat analogates. Analogy is human-relative, and as usual, the humans who interpret reality are hidden in plain sight behind their own interpretations, thus shielding them from responsibility and challenge. The roots of analogy are in human coping with the world, in the three-way structural relationship between individuals, their communities, and the world they live in.

So what is going on in our analogical living when we relate to God? We have seen the beginnings of an answer already, in the work of chapter 2. We interpersonate in all we know and do; we never act *just* as individuals. This much is intramundane, though we are on the threshold of transcendence. We cross that threshold when we still interpersonate after other persons have done all they can or when intramundane other persons are ontologically incapable of providing the troth on which we depend if we are to live at all. The paradigm for this logical move is in D. Z. Phillips, who said that *these* why-questions "are asked, not for want of explanations, but *after* explanations have provided all they can offer."[29] What Phillips said about why-questions that we still ask after answers have done all they can provides the model for us. Incidentally, the two moves are related: answers come from other persons, and the move beyond intramundane persons parallels the move beyond intramundane answers.

In effect, when we are up against the lack of answers and persons to answer, we still treat that void in ways similar to our relating to intramundane persons. It is important to remember both the similarities and dissimilarities, as IV Lateran would counsel. It is *we* who meet the void[30] on a per-

---

[28] Cf. Phillips, *The Concept of Prayer*, 50–51.
[29] Phillips, *The Problem of Evil*, 133–134.
[30] Cf. Niebuhr, *Radical Monotheism*, 122.

sonal basis, even though it is not a person among other persons. To forget that ultimate reality is not simply a person leads to an anthropomorphic conception of God. To forget our own interpersonation toward ultimate reality is to evade responsibility for our own life-shaping acts and commitments. Sometimes we *speak* as to another person, but this is a deliberate category error, undertaken because there is no other way to explain human dependence on transcendence. Analytic philosophy of religion would object, of course, that it is a contradiction to speak this way. But contradiction and category errors are the nerve of irony.[31] Analytic philosophy is hostile to irony; biblical religion is dead without it.

5.6 Acts of God

Asking how we relate to ultimate reality, we inevitably come to acts of God. Human being is the sort of being that copes with the world, and so in coming to ultimate reality, we come to *providence*. To treat the events we handle in coping with life *as* providence is to meet them on a personal level. Hence acts of God. We continue the exploration begun in earnest in *The Accountant's Tale*.[32]

To treat the contingencies of life as providence, as acts of God, does at least three things. (1) It construes them as gifts from a transcendent giver. Whether they are welcome or not is another matter; we struggle with the pains of life and in that struggle we come to God. (That is one of the meanings of "Israel," he who struggles with God.) (2) It construes the transcendent as the ultimate locus of approval or disapproval, and that approval is received in a personal way: it is what matters to a human person in the sense of a blessing (or not). (3) Lastly, to construe events as providential is to meet someone (personal) in them, and that meeting is part of my own constitution *as* a person.

Let me dismantle several traditional but unworkable concepts of both human and divine action.

First, human action. It will be the primary analogate, the analogical prototype for divine action. Beginning with what action is not, the inquiry actually turns up features of any action, not just human action. The model of action that doesn't work very well is taken from a rather casual reading

---

[31] Cf. Mulhall, *Philosophical Myths of the Fall*, 12, cited on p. 40 above.
[32] *The Accountant's Tale*, sec. 8.6, "Acts of God."

of Aristotle, who takes action as motion initiated from within the actor. One place where that definition appears is in *On the Soul*, III.9–10. Aristotle begins not with any word for act or action[33] but, like a good physicist, with motion. It is not a disastrous beginning, if the reader can read between the lines to see what is presupposed along with motion but never spelled out as well as we should like. Aristotle's explanation acknowledges practical reason and thought (along with appetite): "These... appear to be sources of movement: appetite and thought" (433a9–10).[34] Appetite would take us to human interests. Reason and thought implicate language, and in matters of action, narrative. Aristotle focuses on narrative in the *Poetics* but the discussion in *On the Soul* has few links to the *Poetics*. Those of a naturalistic bent (especially in our own time) ignore practical reason and pursue motion to its naturalistic efficient causes, not seeing the role of narrative in the concept of action.

When the thread of practical reason is teased out and narrative appears, we begin to see what action is apart from naturalistic readings of Aristotle. My source was Paul Ricoeur, in *Time and Narrative*, in my own inquiry in *Living in Spin*, chapter 4. What appeared there was a circular relationship between narrative and motions, as well as a human ability to make sense of the world in terms of narrative and practical contingencies. So far as I can see, that ability simply has to be accepted; it is not possible to get behind it or before it and derive it from something more primordial. I would take 'motion' in a practical or existential sense, not the physicist's sense (material trajectories in differential equations). Motion begins to tell what matters; trajectories do not.[35] One cannot begin to talk about an act without already presupposing some idea of the pertinent motions — fragments of a narrative, in effect. The mind (or ideal logic, if you like) goes back and forth between the narrative and the motions, filling in as much detail as is necessary, criticizing the narrative that results until it is adequate.[36] What emerges on reflection is that there are many possible narratives of the act or event. The many narratives do not converge, simply

---

[33] Greek has many words for act and action but they have a range of meaning that is concrete, particular, and colorful compared to the bland, abstract, and comprehensive English verb 'act.'

[34] Unnoticed by Aristotle and his commentators is that he has here combined categories from two very different discourses, physics and the existential experience of human being-in-the-world. See Ricoeur, *Freedom and Nature*, 68 and passim.

[35] Porter, *Living in Spin*, section 6.1.1, "The Problem of Meaning and Motions," for the differences between trajectories, motions, and meaning.

[36] Porter, *Living in Spin*, 125–126.

because there is no way to measure convergence. We criticize in other ways. It can happen that multiple narratives are not even close to one another. An example was conjured in *Spin* (pp. 144–145), of someone purchasing sundries in a convenience store in an act that turned out to be many acts — in the end, too many to find and count. And so, with all due respect to The Philosopher's sense of practical reason, we have come to what action is. An "action happens when some contingency affects someone's interests and is narratable."[37] *Spin* focused on human action, but our interest here is in divine action.

Second, divine action: it is not interference with otherwise natural motions of bodies in the world; in a word, "miracles."[38] This concept of divine action comes from a naturalistic reading of Aristotle: an act is a species of caused motion. That definition was pursued in a naturalistic direction, ignoring Aristotle's allusions to practical reason, and it has shaped discussion of divine action in the modern period. My term for it was 'volokinesis' in *Where, Now, O Biologists?*, a polemic against creationism as one species of theology of divine action by interference with nature.[39] The unexpected and the unexplained are not volokinesis nor violations of natural laws, though the unexpected and unexplained may contribute to a clearing in which we can see ultimate reality show itself. In any case, they are human-relative, not "objective" at all.

Having ruled out some of what divine action is not, look at what divine action is. We come to divine action when we attend to some narratable contingency in a personal way, even though there are no persons to relate to in the contingency of interest. This is the threshold of transcendence. Since questioning into transcendence can be focused on any contingency, divine action is in everything. Nevertheless, rarely do we focus on everything all at once, and even when we do, we do not inquire into much detail; we just ask about "the world" taken as a whole. More interesting are clearings, places in life where our questioning runs beyond particular persons or causes. In such a clearing, we can see ultimate reality show itself in the world.

---

[37] Porter, *Living in Spin*, 5.

[38] This was discussed at length in *The Accountant's Tale*, chapter 8. The literature is vast, and beyond the scope of this study.

[39] The whole book was a polemic against volokinesis, but the section on divine action in *Where, Now, O Biologists* (chapter 8) dealt *only* with volokinesis, leaving issues of narrative and interpersonation for later.

To characterize an event or contingency as an act of God is a way of relating to it on a personal level. Even though God does not "exist," he does act. Here, as far as possible, we refrain from equivocating on the meanings of *exist*.

The whole point of volokinesis as an explanation of divine action is to validate ultimate rejection of Limitation. Volokinesis supposedly objectivates acts of God, thereby "proving" them. Real volokinesis would spook people beyond measure, and so make them more anxious, not less, but pretend volokinesis tranquilizes anxiety very effectively, especially when it is hidden long ago and far away. Among the uses of something objective is that it can be shown to other people (whether they are present or not). And so the "objective" is interpersonal, and its anxiolytic power depends on the possibility of other people, but other people hidden from view, so that they may comfort without challenging. Objectivity is a form of responsibility, but its abuses work precisely as a way of getting *out* of responsibility.

5.7 Ambiguity and Creaturehood

We began with a parody of the prolog to the Gospel of John. It can be heard in many ways, and I hope it is reverent but neither flippant nor pious. How to read it depends on how we see ourselves in the world and in relation to God. There are many complaints in the Bible, complaints expressing John Courtney Murray's first question of God, "Where is he when we need him?" Better, "Where were you when we needed you?," as in Pss. 89 and 44, among others. Answers are open, for we never know in full. If the Joke is taken as in some sense benevolent,[40] it means hearing the parody of John in quite another key. That claim in somewhat more pious language is in Isaiah,

> My thoughts are not your thoughts,
> my ways are not your ways (55.8, JB).

Some jokes should not be explained and not explaining them sharpens their challenge. On the other hand, not explaining carries great risks, and it seems better to me to indicate some links to the tradition that would make sense of the irony and ambiguity within which we live. The question, in

---

[40] Remember that you can declare any kind of covenant with ultimate reality you like, but ultimate reality will interpret it as it pleases, not as you do.

terms of H. Richard Niebuhr's short essay, "Faith in Gods and in God,"[41] is about how to relate to the void from which we come and with which (or with whom) we all have to deal. "The causes for which we live all die": hence that void. It begins as indifferent or an enemy and ends as a friend and companion in our pilgrimage through history. In another light, this is called creaturehood. Reinhold Niebuhr put it this way:

> The Christian view of man ... affirms that the evil in man is a consequence of his inevitable though not necessary unwillingness to acknowledge his dependence, to accept his finiteness and to admit his insecurity, an unwillingness which involves him in the vicious circle of accentuating the insecurity from which he seeks escape.[42]

One way to acknowledge our creaturehood without in that very act trying to evade that creaturehood is to say, "In the beginning was the Joke and the Joke was on us," and mean it with warmth, gratitude, and reverence. It can be done. The fact that it can also be heard as flippant is itself an instance of the Joke, i.e., of the very ambiguity of language in which we live and from which we would like to escape. That is itself an inescapable part of our creaturehood. It comes with the ambiguity of language and of human interests.

To construct a General Theory of The Joke would answer questions that are legitimate and doubtless worthy, especially in regard to the relationship between human being, ontology, and the ambiguity of language. It would also afford a way of trying to get control over our own creaturehood. Furthermore, some would use it to answer unanswerable questions, with all the mischief that entails.

We have returned to the problem with which we began, ambiguity in human actions and human lives. If they are ambiguous, what saves us from the kind of failure that would seem to be inherent in ambiguity? If lives and actions are not well defined, how can they be good, forgiven, redeemed, worthy (or not)? Sometimes we can resolve ambiguity for limited purposes, but it is always possible to expand the horizon of interest and find ambiguity again. What is more, we do not know the ambiguity

---

[41] Niebuhr, *Radical Monotheism*, 122.

[42] Reinhold Niebuhr, *The Nature and Destiny of Man*, vol. I, *Human Nature*, 150, chapter VI, the beginning and ending of the opening paragraph. One could find a perfect illustration for Reinhold Niebuhr's point in the *Far Side* cartoons of Gary Larson.

5.7 Ambiguity and Creaturehood

introduced by our own language, in contrast to language as it might be for some other species. Why should our own languages be privileged?

That is the sort of reason why the tradition looked to Judgement Day. On Judgement Day, all ambiguities will be resolved, there are answers to questions about our lives and actions, and we can know those answers. Yet Judgement Day was always looked to with a certain measured dread, even when approached with sure and certain hope. We do not know all about ourselves, not now, and not in any way that could guarantee knowledge in principle.

Judgement selects among possible narratives the ones that are true. Truth is always built on troth and so we are dependent on the troth of ultimate reality. Editing narratives is a corporate activity, in which we are dependent on others and in the end, on an Other beyond all others, even when that Other is not a being that could "exist." We can appeal to that Other, sometimes with, sometimes against all others. The ambiguity of so many possible narratives is wide enough to include some that give us narratives in which we can be at home. How can that be? This demands some sort of honesty; answers cannot just be fabricated.

What can make answers both true and effective? Foils, as *Living in Spin* said: other stories, stories that shape the ones we live in; especially human suffering, in which we see the presence of ultimate reality here with us. Others' suffering both judges and saves. Is there proof? No, there is no proof. We are dependent on grace.

Chapter 6

Some Sort of Ending

6.1 A Few Answers

A few questions recur over and over again in this inquiry:

>What is your proposed basic life orientation?
>>Your idea of ultimate reality?
>
>Where does it show itself in life and the world?
>What story do you *want* to be a part of?
>What story *are* you a part of?
>How do you want to handle the pains of life?
>Is human life just part of nature,
>>or does history matter?

The answers have to be confessional, not derived, for we are talking about starting points, which cannot be reasoned *to*. Biblical answers are not universally shared. For only one example, we have a focus on history and narrative, but a Buddhist friend of mine once quipped, "We think the whole point is to get *beyond* narrative."

Some short summary answers to the questions above:

>We affirm human life in this world as good,
>in full view of its pains,
>and in that affirmation
>we place our lives in history,
>with enough transcendence
>to deal with (but not pretend to answer)
>>unanswerable questions
>>that arise in this engagement with life.

6.1 A Few Answers

More is incorporated by reference in this short creed than is obvious. It is methodological as much as substantive. How did we come to affirm human life in this world as good? That happened in history, and in a sense, the history happened to us, even though we choose it and could have chosen differently.

Within biblical religion, Christians and Jews do not do this in entirely the same way, but it is important for Christians to acknowledge the degree and depth of our agreements and our common debts to Second Temple Judaism. Obviously, I cannot speak for rabbinic Judaism in what follows. Indeed, it will be only with great luck that the present explanations do adequate justice to my own side of biblical religion, Christianity. For Christians, meeting God comes first in particular persons in a historical tradition, Jesus focally, but not solely. Christian answers to the questions above must sooner or later come to Christology: How is transcendence present in the person of Jesus of Nazareth? What do those events *do* for Christians today? The questions ask about the Person and the Work of Christ. The doctrine of the Work of Christ was never regulated, though the Person of Christ was (as at Chalcedon). There have been many explanations of the Work of Christ, and none can claim authority to the exclusion of all the others. The present comments are only one more and doubtless not the last. And even Chalcedon under-determines explanations of the Person of Christ, the Incarnation.[1]

When asked where does our ultimate reality show itself in the world, we answer focally with the events of Jesus, especially the Passion. But just as the Passion gets its meaning only from its context in the Gospels, Jesus gets his meaning from his place in the inheritance from the Common Documents, Second Temple Judaism, and their place in the larger history of religions. In other words, the Work of Christ gets its meaning from its place in Exodus typology; it is not a starting point on its own. In recent centuries, Exodus typology has been forgotten. The problem became just sin, viewed without any particular use for the Exodus. Exodus typology survives unrecognized in the Gospels, especially the Synoptics, but it was downgraded already in the Marcionite crisis of the second century. It is often lost in modern theology.

---

[1] The present inquiry will not stumble into an explanation of the Person of Christ, because too many other questions need to be answered first. Nevertheless, it is fair to stipulate that if I ever write about the Person of Christ, it will be thoroughly Chalcedonian.

6.2 The Work of Christ

There is more about the Work of Christ in *Living in Spin* (sections 7.1.3 and 7.2.1), and so the remarks here will be brief and somewhat summary. Edward Hobbs once said in instructional materials,

> ... suffering for others (both because of others and for the sake of) others is what God does. Suffering for others is part of the calling of those who would share in God's life ($\zeta\omega\acute{\eta}$ $\alpha\acute{\iota}\acute{\omega}\nu\iota o\varsigma$).[2]

I accept his reading of the Gospels, but it is not only God who suffers because of and for the sake of others; we all do. That, of course, is why this suffering, the Passion, is part of the answer to "Where does your proposed ultimate reality show itself in the world, in history?" We don't always have to suffer for others; some of it is voluntary and can be evaded. That is why Hobbs went on to say,

> Jesus summons others to follow him to Calvary (suffering and sacrifice), to share in his life.

If human life includes suffering for others, and if we are to affirm human life in this world in full view of its pains, then suffering has to be dealt with positively, it has to be fitted into a good world and a good life.

One might well ask, Why *this* suffering? For as horrible as it was, others have suffered more. The Passion is chosen as the principal clearing because of its role in the history of biblical religion, and because of how it advances that history. Christian answers at this point are different from rabbinic answers, but the rabbis have their own ways of dealing with this problem. What occupies us now are Christian answers. The treatment of suffering grows in the sequence Qoheleth, Job, deutero-Isaiah (particularly the Servant Songs), and the Gospels.[3] It is not as if the Gospels alone complete the sequence, for the Pauline theology of the Body of Christ stands in a similar relation to the older documents. The Body of Christ is corporate, just as the Servant of deutero-Isaiah is corporate, and both play

---

[2] Edward Hobbs, in an untitled list of "Seven Hallmarks of the Canonical Gospels." Italics removed.

[3] See Samuel Terrien, introduction to Job in the *Interpreter's Bible* vol. III, cols. 889a–890a for the placement of Job before deutero-Isaiah. Terrien cites R. H. Pfeiffer, among others.

the role of all Israel. Pauline theology is easily upstaged by the Gospels but it should not be.

The Passion gets its place in this sequence from Exodus typology.[4] In both the Exodus and its retrieval in the Gospels, after a period of activity, Israel (or Jesus) goes up to Jerusalem for its/his final triumph. How that triumph is to be interpreted has a certain ambiguity, though I think the Gospels make their own reading clear, as I argued in *The Accountant's Tale* on the Resurrection. Is the Resurrection a separate event or is it originally an interpretation of the Passion? Does the Resurrection promise us a way out of Limitation or does it offer us a new perspective (*metanoia*) on finding salvation *in* Limitation? In my reading (and Hobbs's), we are to find salvation in Limitation rather than in ultimately getting out of it. Readers usually start by trying to get out of Limitation and progress only slowly to making peace with it in a change of perspective on themselves, life, and the world.

Some observations. World-affirming historical religion exists, and you can join it if you like, but there is more than just that in the Work of Christ. What does the Passion *do* to and for believers? This is an ontological question. The believer is transformed by the Passion; he becomes a different person. This line of inquiry turns on how we conceive human action and human lives. The preparation for some answers was laid down in *Living in Spin*.

One act or event can reconstitute another. To borrow some traditional language, one act can reconstitute the formal causes of others; possibly final causes also, but *Spin* went beyond the traditional Aristotelian schema. The classic example is in King Lear, the foil of Kent and his sons which shows us what is going on with Lear and his daughters.[5] We don't know what somebody is doing until we know the relevant context, which invites the question, what makes some features relevant and others irrelevant? Sometimes that question can be answered, sometimes it is just ambiguous. Sometimes it is chosen.

In *Spin* we saw examples of the agent patient, one who suffers and thereby acts on the lives of people around him.[6] During the Nazi period, a few students, known together as the White Rose, distributed anti-Nazi tracts. For this, they were executed. They said more in their dying than in

---

[4] Porter, *The Accountant's Tale*, section 3.1.
[5] Porter, *Living in Spin*, section 5.2.4, "Ontological Foils."
[6] Porter, *Living in Spin*, section 5.3.3.

their writing. Their texts have come and gone; their dying transformed the people around them, whether those people knew about them or not. And the White Rose is only one example among many.

We saw a perversely inverted example of the same logic when the American presidential assassins have to beg Lee Harvey Oswald to go through with it (he was hesitant, in Sondheim and Weidman's play *Assassins*).[7] It is a grotesque parody, of course, but it is solid philosophy of action:

> Through you and your act
>> we dare to hope ...
>
> Through you and your act
>> we are revived and given meaning ...
>
> Our lives, our acts, are given meaning
> Today we are reborn, through you.[8]

Both the assassins and the Gospels appeal to foils that change their lives. But who is right? The assassins, or the Gospels?

The ambiguity can be dealt with, but it is real nonetheless. The Gospels deal with it explicitly, in the Words of Institution the night before the Passion. In the liturgical version, which is reworked from Mark 14.22–25 and 1 Cor 11.24–25, Jesus says of the bread,

> Take this, all of you, and eat it:
> this is my body which will be given up for you.

And of the wine:

> Take this, all of you, and drink from it:
> this is the cup of my blood,
> the blood of the everlasting covenant.
> It will be shed for you and for all
> so that sins may be forgiven.
> Do this in memory of me.[9]

The liturgical text spells out that the bread is (1) the Lord's *body*, (2) given *for you* (and for all, incidentally), (3) the initiation of a new covenant, (4)

---

[7] Porter, *Living in Spin*, section 2.2.5, "Through you and your act."

[8] Porter, *Living in Spin*, 30; Sondheim and Weidman, *Assassins*, 100–102.

[9] Catholic Church, *The Book of Divine Worship*, 363, Holy Eucharist, Rite Two.

6.2 The Work of Christ

so that sins may be forgiven, and (5) in memory of me. All five of these words have more meaning in the distributed ontology of action explored in *Spin* than they do in the ontology of secular culture or mainstream philosophy.

(1) The Body of Christ is at home in radical interpersonation but not in modern naturalism, nominalism, materialism, or individualism. It is for Paul a natural way of speaking but it is not philosophy. Modern instincts in philosophy are a very effective way of evading interpersonation. Paul's theology does, however, make good sense in the perspective that takes human being as always involving other human beings.

(2) The text defines the act as *for you*, which is a lot more than the modern worldview can handle. It happens often enough that one person suffers because of or for the sake of another, but what we have in mind when we say that presupposes that they are both parts of one story. We don't trouble to ask in narrative theory what makes the parts parts of one story; we have colloquial narrative skills that do that for us. What is intended here in the Words of Institution and the Work of Christ that they invoke is something bigger. The Passion of Christ, in one story, transforms what happens in every other story. The Passion is a foil for all the other stories. In another sense, we are all part of a larger story, one that includes the Passion. We tell as much of that larger story as we need at present. "Men have found no better thing than this to do"[10] to mark the relationship between this clearing and the events of the moment. Ultimate reality shows itself here and so illuminates everything else, before and after.

(3) The New Covenant could not have been clear at the time but in hindsight it is obvious.[11] This text does more than proclaim it; it *constitutes* it. The declarative speech act is ontological.

(4) "So that sins may be forgiven" indicates that human actions are quite transformed by the presence of ultimate reality in this clearing. Members of the human species are singularly dissatisfied with their own behavior. From this grows the sense of sin for which the text proclaims forgiveness. It is more than particular acts, it is a condition of human personhood in the world. The remedy lies in human suffering for and with one another, and the Passion is the exemplary clearing in which ultimate reality shows itself.

(5) Jesus is quoted to say "do this in memory of me," for the

---

[10] Dix, *The Shape of the Liturgy*, 743–745. The text has been quoted on the Net.

[11] See remarks on Aphrahat in Porter, *The Accountant's Tale*, 214.

ἀνάμνησις of me. More than just mere memory is at stake in ἀνάμνησις, for the liturgical act makes ontologically present the original Passion, in one act spread throughout all history. For liturgists this is ontological but philosophers are strangely unenthusiastic about it.

In effect, the Passion reconstitutes me as having-been-suffered-for, through its action as a foil for my own life. This is less painful than any of my own small pains but it is far more galling. The liturgical and biblical texts emphasize the gall by using the (abhorrent) image of cannibalism. If I live, it is at the cost of others' suffering, the Passion focally. This is the form that having-a-stake-in-other-persons takes for Christians.

6.3 Some Foils

In a story told in the Bavli, Moses and God are talking.[12] Moses asks a question about Torah and to answer, God puts him in the back of Rabbi Akiba's classroom. Moses does not understand. A lot has happened to the Torah since it was given to Moses.

Moses asks, "Such Torah! Such teaching! Show me his end!" God shows him. Rabbi Akiba died in the Second Jewish Revolt, of 135 CE, in the siege of Jerusalem, butchered and sold for meat in the famine of the siege.

To try to turn this suffering into something redemptive for all time would turn the stomach. It would be worse than gilding a lily, which is often what has been done to the Passion. Would Akiba's suffering, if placed in a narrative context shaped by Exodus typology, be as plausible as Jesus' suffering? I can't say.

The point is made by the events of the Shoah. After ten centuries of escalating anti-Jewish violence and murder, the worst was in the Destruction of European Jewry.[13] Jews and others have rightly protested against attempts to defang the challenge of the Shoah by construing it as redemptive suffering. The Shoah stands as a challenge to Christians, who begot the culture out of which the Shoah came. It is a witness against sacred canopies, a witness against the bad faith that hides and evades the responsibility for the socially constructed reality that is the Incarnation.

The Shoah presents at least two challenges to Christian theology: In the first place, the lesson of a responsible liberty of interpretation given

---

[12] The story is in Menahoth, 29b. Soncino edition, Seder Kodashim 1, 190.

[13] The worst so far. Many today would like to repeat the Shoah and finish what it began.

also to rabbinic Judaism has not yet been learned by Christian theology. That is simple enough, though its corollary is harder. The second lesson is that the Incarnation is both true and also a matter of choice. Chalcedon is at stake. In the terms of the Definition, the Incarnation in its worldly φύσις is accessible to sociology and the history of religions, for both of which it is a matter of choice. It is a social construction. So what does it mean to confess that *God* was present in Jesus, reconciling the world to himself in the Incarnation? The Incarnation is a clearing in which it is possible to see ultimate reality. As with all social constructions, clearings in particular, we are at the mercy of ultimate reality when we claim that our social constructions host the presence of ultimate reality.

One guess may be hazarded. If harm comes again to rabbinic Judaism through the Church's action OR INACTION, the Church could easily be rendered morally bankrupt.[14] It could become impossible to continue a Christology that the "tradition" would recognize as acceptable.

6.4 Kyrie Eleison

In *Unwelcome Good News*, section 6.1, I said that ultimate reality really does enter into our human social constructions, as an adult enters into children's games. But we have no control over it. More than once I have said that you can erect any kind of covenant you want with ultimate reality, but be very, very careful: ultimate reality may not interpret your covenant in exactly the way you thought it would.

With apologies to Paul Tillich and the Novus Ordo, in the words of the Mass, slightly altered,

> Ultimate Reality, we are not worthy
> that you should enter
>   into our human socially constructed realities,
> but only say the word, and we shall be healed.

Healed: made whole. What does it mean to be made whole? We never completely know. That is one of the consequences of the distributed on-

---

[14] It could easily become bankrupt for lesser offenses, if archbishops are not held accountable for abusing altar boys and seminarians but that issue is beyond this book. Some say the Church already is bankrupt, for both these and other reasons, but I hold out some hope for reform.

tology. Incomplete knowledge is the most that is given to us, this side of final Judgement. What that might be, we really don't know.

What is the word to be said, that we may be healed? For philosophers and theologians? The word is *grace*. We are dependent upon grace. It is inherent in the nature of transcendence that it cannot be demonstrated — and that puts us at the mercy of grace. We have no control over it, not even the conceptual control of proofs.

One consequence of the ambiguity of our socially constructed realities should be noted with a little emphasis. The liturgy is full of pleas for mercy. The Kyrie is only one of the more conspicuous. Before the issue of sin is even raised, we ask for mercy precisely because we do not know what we are doing, we do not know the larger narratives of which we are a part, we do not know the ambiguities we live in, we do not know all the other narratives that might make better sense of our lives, we do not know ... there is so much we do not know.

Put it another way: Our socially constructed realities have no claim on ultimate reality. Hence the plea above.

All that is before we look at our own disappointing actions. Typically, when a human life appears to have some narrative coherence, there are parts that are regrettable, sometimes large, structural parts. Those disappointments go unresolved — in "this life." Here the dirty incoherences and ironies of our lives cry out for transcendence, some healing for the narratives that we *do* have. Such a soul craves purgatory.

We are always torn between the two despairs: Here, the despair of self-assertion takes the form of proofs and sacred canopies; the despair of apathy takes the form of postmodern nihilism, giving up on truth and retreating into the cynicism of will to power. (The two despairs are closer to one another than they might seem.) Both are everywhere available today. Real hope — like real transcendence — cannot prove itself. It is easy to point to places in life where the opportunity for hope is clear enough, but it remains a choice. The alternative in despair eventually shows itself as depravity, whether banal or grandiose, whether in absurdity or in atrocities. Though depravity's repulsiveness is never proof, it is demanding nonetheless: it puts us to the question, and that question gets answered, one way or another, in how we respond.

We are in the world of The Joke, the Joke is on us, and we never entirely understand. Does it underwrite truth? Yes, but not a Platonist truth, not an unambiguous truth that we could comprehend or control. Does it allow any meaning for human action? Yes, though no cause for which humans act lives forever (*Radical Monotheism*, p. 122). Does it love us? Is it here, with us? I trust so — but in saying that, I am shooting my mouth off. That is no more than acknowledging my (and our) dependence on grace.

Bibliography

Augustine of Hippo. *The Literal Meaning of Genesis*, 2 vols. Trans. John Hammond Taylor SJ. New York: Paulist Press, 1982.

Ballard, James G. *Empire of the Sun*. London: V. Gollancz, 1984. See also the movie directed by Steven Spielberg.

Beck, Norman. *Mature Christianity in the 21st Century; the Recognition and Repudiation of the Anti-Jewish Polemic of the New Testament*. New York: Crossroad, 1994.

Berger, Peter L. *A Rumor of Angels: Modern Society and the Rediscovery of the Supernatural*, New York: Doubleday, 1969; 2nd ed., 1990.

Berger, Peter L. *The Sacred Canopy: Elements of a Sociological Theory of Religion*. New York: Doubleday, 1967.

Berger, Peter L., and Thomas Luckmann. *The Social Construction of Reality; A Treatise in the Sociology of Knowledge*. New York: Doubleday, 1966.

Blair, Alexander. "Christian Ambivalence Toward the Old Testament: a correlation among some issues in philosophy, theology, and biblical studies." Berkeley, CA: Graduate Theological Union. PhD Diss., 1984.

Blair, Alexander, *Christian Ambivalence Toward Its Old Testament: Interactive Creativity versus Static Obedience*. Eugene, OR: Wipf and Stock, 2010.

Brague, Rémi. *Eccentric Culture: a Theory of Western Civilization.* Trans. Samuel Lester. South Bend, Ind.: St. Augustine's Press, 2002.

Brook, Peter, director, *Lord of the Flies.* Movie released in 1963.

Brueggemann, Walter and Hans Walter Wolff. *The Vitality of Old Testament Traditions.* Atlanta: John Knox Press, 1975.

Buber, Martin. *Between Man and Man.* Mansfield Center, CT: Martino Publishing, 2014. Originally published in German in 1938.

Bultmann, Rudolf. *The Gospel of John: A Commentary.* Philadelphia: Westminster, 1971.

Burrell, David B. *Knowing the Unknowable God: Ibn-Sina, Maimonides, Aquinas.* Notre Dame: University of Notre Dame Press, 1986.

Catholic Church. *Fides et Ratio.* Encyclical of John Paul II, 1998-09-14. http://www.vatican.va/content/john-paul-ii/en/encyclicals/documents/hf_jp-ii_enc_14091998_fides-et-ratio.html

Catholic Church. The Oath Against Modernism, 1910. Available online at http://www.papalencyclicals.net/Pius10/p10moath.htm.

Catholic Church, the National Council of Catholic Bishops. *The Book of Divine Worship.* Mt. Pocono, PA: Newman House Press, 2003. The subtitle reads: "Being elements of the Book of Common Prayer revised and adapted according to the Roman Rite for use by Roman Catholics coming from the Anglican tradition."

Coffey, David. "The Whole Rahner on the Supernatural Existential." *Theological Studies* 65 (2004) 95–118.

Collingwood, Robin George. *An Autobiography.* Oxford: Oxford University Press, 1939.

Collingwood, Robin George. *An Essay on Metaphysics.* Oxford: Oxford University Press, 1940.

Damasio, Antonio. *Descartes' Error: Emotion, Reason and the Human Brain.* New York: Avon, 1995.

Dix, Gregory, OSB. *The Shape of the Liturgy*. London: Dacre Press, 1944.

Dreyfus, Hubert L. *Being-in-the-World: A Commentary on Heidegger's "Being and Time," Division I*. Cambridge, MA: MIT Press, 1991.

Dreyfus, Hubert L. *What Computers Still Can't Do; A Critique of Artificial Reason*. Third edition. Cambridge, MA: MIT Press, 1992.

Dupré, Louis. *Passage to Modernity; an Essay in the Hermeneutics of Nature and Culture*. New Haven: Yale University Press, 1993.

Eliade, Mircea. *Cosmos and History; or The Myth of the Eternal Return. Le Mythe de l'Éternel retour: archétypes et répétition*. Paris: Gallimard, 1949. Trans. Willard Trask. New York: Harper, 1959.

Ellis, John M. *Language, Thought, and Logic*. Evanston: Northwestern University Press, 1993.

Epstein, I., ed., *The Babylonian Talmud*. London: Soncino Press, 1948.

Fingarette, Herbert. *Self Deception*. London: RKP, 1969. Second edition, Berkeley and Los Angeles: University of California Press, 2000.

Franks, Curtis. "The Realm of the Sacred, wherein we may not draw an inference from something which itself has been inferred, a reading of Talmud Bavli Zevachim folio 50." Preprint at one of Curtis Franks' web-sites.

Gadamer, Hans-Georg. *Truth and Method*. Second edition, Trans. Joel Weinsheimer and Donald G. Marshall. New York: Crossroad, 1989. The German original, *Wahrheit und Methode*, was published in 1960.

Golding, William. *Darkness Visible*. London: Faber and Faber, 1979.

Golding, William. Lord of the Flies. London: Faber and Faber, 1954; and later editions. See also the movie directed by Peter Brook.

Hamilton, A. G. *Numbers, Sets, and Axioms: the Apparatus of Mathematics*. Cambridge University Press, 1983.

Heidegger, Martin. *Introduction to Metaphysics*. Trans. Ralph Mannheim. New Haven: Yale University Press, 1959.

Heidegger, Martin. *Sein und Zeit*, 1927. *Being and Time*. Trans. John Macquarrie and Edward Robinson. New York: Harper and Row, 1960. There is also a translation by Joan Stambaugh (Albany: State University of New York Press, 1996). Unless otherwise noted, references are to the Macquarrie and Robinson translation.

Heidegger, Martin. *The Fundamental Concepts of Metaphysics: World, Finitude, Solitude*. Trans. William McNeill and Nicholas Walker. Bloomington: Indiana University Press, 1995. The German was published in 1983.

Heidegger, Martin. "The Origin of the Work of Art." In *Poetry, Language, Thought*, ed. Albert Hofstadter. New York: Harper and Row, 1975.

Hemming, Laurence Paul and Susan Frank Parsons, eds. *Restoring Faith in Reason*, a translation of *Fides et Ratio*. London: SCM and Notre Dame: University of Notre Dame Press, 2002.

Hobbs, Edward C. "An Alternate Model from a Theological Perspective." In Herbert A. Otto, *The Family in Search of a Future*. New York: Appleton-Century-Crofts, 1970.

Hobbs, Edward C. "Eight Interpretations of the Significance of the Evangelists' Use of Old Testament Models in Interpreting Jesus." Unpublished instructional materials from the late 1970s.

Hobbs, Edward C. Lectures in Houston, no. 4: "Can an apocalyptic prophet make sense in century 21?" Foundation for Contemporary Theology, March 23, 2002.

Iggers, Georg G. *The German Conception of History: The National Tradition of Historical Thought from Herder to the Present*. Middletown, CT: Wesleyan University Press, 1968, 1983.

Iggers, Georg G. *Historiography In The Twentieth Century; From Scientific Objectivity to the Postmodern Challenge*. Middletown, CT: Wesleyan University Press, 1997.

Jaspers, Karl. *Philosophy*, 3 vols. University of Chicago Press, 1969–1971.

John of Damascus. *The Exposition of The Orthodox Faith*. Trans. S. D. F. Salmond in the nineteenth century; Aeterna Press, 2016. The Greek is in Migne, *Patrologia Graeca*, vol. 94.

Kaufman, Gordon D. *Essay on Theological Method*. Atlanta: Scholars Press, 1990.

Kenny, Anthony. "Aquinas and Wittgenstein." *Downside Review* 77 (1959) 217.

Kierkegaard, Søren. *The Sickness Unto Death. A Christian Psychological Exposition for Understanding and Awakening*. Walter Lowrie, trans. Princeton: Princeton University Press, 1955.

Kierkegaard, Søren. *The Sickness Unto Death. A Christian Psychological Exposition for Understanding and Awakening*. Trans. Howard V. Hong and Edna H. Hong. Princeton: Princeton University Press, 1980.

Krentz, Edgar. *The Historical-Critical Method*. Philadelphia: Fortress Press, 1975.

Kuhn, Thomas S. *The Structure of Scientific Revolutions*. Second edition. Chicago: University of Chicago Press, 1970. The first edition was published in 1960.

Lakoff, George. *Women, Fire, and Dangerous Things*. Chicago: University of Chicago Press, 1987.

MacIntyre, Alasdair. *After Virtue*. Third Edition. Notre Dame: University of Notre Dame, Press, 2007.

MacIntyre, Alasdair C. "Epistemological Crises, Dramatic Narrative, and the Philosophy of Science." *Monist* 60 no. 4 (1977/10) 453–472.

MacIntyre, Alasdair. "Relativism, Power, and Philosophy." *Proceedings and Addresses of the American Philosophical Association* 59 no. 1 (1985/September) 5; reprinted in K. Baynes, J. Bohman and T. McCarthy, eds., *After Philosophy*, MIT Press, 1987, pp. 385–411.

MacIntyre, Alasdair. *Whose Justice? Which Rationality?* Notre Dame: University of Notre Dame Press, 1988.

Mascal, E. L. *The Openness of Being: Natural Theology Today*. London: Darton Longman and Todd, 1971. The Gifford Lectures, 1970–71.

Mead, George Herbert. *Mind, Self and Society; From the Standpoint of Social Behaviorist*. Chicago: University of Chicago Press, 1934.

Midrash Rabbah Genesis. vol. one, trans. Rabbi H. Freedman. Third edition. London and New York: Soncino Press, 1983.

Mulhall, Stephen. *Philosophical Myths of the Fall*. Princeton University Press, 2005.

Murray, John Courtney, S.J. *The Problem of God*. New Haven: Yale University Press, 1964.

Myers, Doris T. *C. S. Lewis in Context*. Kent, Ohio: Kent State University Press, 1994.

Nédoncelle, Maurice. "Prosopon et persona dans l'antiquité classique." *Revue des sciences religieuses* 22 (1948) 277–299.

Niebuhr, H. Richard. *Radical Monotheism and Western Culture, with Supplementary Essays*. New York: Harper and Row, 1970.

Niebuhr, H. Richard. *The Meaning of Revelation* (Originally published circa 1940). Third edition. Louisville: Westminster John Knox Press, 2006. Citations unless otherwise noted are to the third edition.

Niebuhr, H. Richard. *The Responsible Self. An Essay in Christian Moral Philosophy*. New York: Harper and Row, 1963.

Niebuhr, H. Richard. *Faith on Earth; An Inquiry into the Structure of Human Faith*. New Haven: Yale University Press, 1989.

Niebuhr, Reinhold. *The Nature and Destiny of Man*. Two volumes. New York: Scribners, 1941.

O'Callaghan, John. "Can We Demonstrate that 'God Exists'?" *Nova et Vetera* 14 no. 2 (2016) 619–644.

Phillips, D. Z. *The Concept of Prayer*. London: Routledge and Kegan Paul, 1965.

Phillips, D. Z. *The Problem of Evil and the Problem of God*. Minneapolis: Fortress Press, 2004.

Pieper, Josef. *On Hope* San Francisco: Ignatius Press, 1986.

Placher, William V. *The Domestication of Transcendence: How Modern Thinking about God went wrong*. Louisville, KY: Westminster John Knox Press, c1996.

Porter, Andrew P. *Basic Concepts of Biblical Religion; A Prolegomenon*. Xulon Press, 2016.

Porter, Andrew P. *Elementary Monotheism*, two volumes. Lanham, MD: University Press of America, 2001.

Porter, Andrew P., and Edward C. Hobbs. "The Trinity and the Indo-European Tripartite Worldview," *Budhi* (Manila) Vol. 3, nos. 2&3 (1999) 1–28. Available on the internet at http://www.jedp.com/trinity.html.

Porter, Andrew P. *Living in Spin: Narrative as a Distributed Ontology of Human Action*. Bloomington, IN: Authorhouse, 2011.

Porter, Andrew P. *Unwelcome Good News: Providence in Human Life*. Eugene, OR: Wipf and Stock, 2004.

Porter, Andrew. *Where, Now, O Biologists, Is Your Theory? Intelligent Design as Naturalism By Other Means*. Eugene, OR: Wipf and Stock, 2007.

Queneau, Raymond. *Exercises in Style*. Trans. Babara Wright. London: John Calder, 1979. The French original was published by Gallimard, 1947.

von Rad, Gerhard. "The Form Critical Problem of the Hexateuch" (1938). Reprinted and translated in *The Problem of the Hexateuch and Other Essays*. London: SCM, 1966.

Raff, Rudolf A. *The Shape of Life: Genes, Development, and the Evolution of Animal Form*. University of Chicago Press, 1996.

Rahner, Karl SJ. "Concerning the Relationship Between Nature and Grace." Trans. Cornelius Ernst. *Theological Investigations* 1 (1961)

297–317, as cited in David Coffey's footnote no. 1. Original "Über das Verhältnis von Natur und Gnade." *Schriften zur Theologie* (Einsiedeln: Benziger, 1954), pp. 323–345. An earlier version was "Eine Antwort," *Orientierung* 14 (1950) 141–145.

Rahner, Karl SJ. *Foundations of Christian Faith: An Introduction to the idea of Christianity*. Trans. William V. Dych. New York: Seabury Press, 1978.

Reagan, Charles E. "Ricoeur's Diagnostic Relation." *International Philosophical Quarterly*, 8 (1968) 586–592.

Ricoeur, Paul. *Freedom and Nature: the Voluntary and the Involuntary*. Evanston: Northwestern University Press, 1966.

Ricoeur, Paul. "The Model of Text: Meaningful Action Considered as Text." *Social Research*, 38 no. 3 (Autumn 1971) 529–555. Reprinted in Paul Ricoeur, *From Text to Action; Essays in Hermeneutics, II*. Trans. Kathleen Blamey and John B. Thompson. Evanston: Northwestern University Press, 1991.

Ricoeur, Paul. *The Symbolism of Evil*. Boston: Beacon Press, 1967.

Ricoeur, Paul. *Time and Narrative*. Three volumes. Chicago: University of Chicago Press, 1984–1985.

Rocca, Gregory. "Aquinas on God-Talk: Hovering Over the Abyss." *Theological Studies* 54 (1993) 641.

Rocca, Gregory. *Speaking the Incomprehensible God; Thomas Aquinas on the Interplay of Positive and Negative Theology*. Catholic University of America Press, 2004.

Rubenstein, Richard L. *After Auschwitz; History, Theology, and Contemporary Judaism*. 2nd ed., Baltimore, Johns Hopkins University Press, 1992.

Sheehan, Thomas. *Making Sense of Heidegger: A Paradigm Shift*. New York: Rowman and Littlefield, 2015.

Sheehan, Thomas. "What, after all, was Heidegger about?" *Continental Philosophy Review* 47:2 (2014). Published online,

2014 October 29. http://religiousstudies.stanford.edu/people/tom-sheehan/publications/.

Spielberg, Steven, *Empire of the Sun*, movie, released in 1987.

Steiner, George. *Real Presences*. University of Chicago Press, 1989.

Strack, Hermann L., and G. Stemberger, *Introduction to the Talmud and Midrash*. ET Markus Bockmuehl; Augsburg Fortress, 1992. There were earlier editions.

Terrien, Samuel. Introduction to Job, in *The Interpreter's Bible*, vol. III.

Thomas Aquinas. *In quator libros sententiarum*. There are many editions, some online. For the Latin of 1.8.1.1 ad 4, I probably consulted E. M. Macierowski, ed., *Thomas Aquinas's Earliest Treatment of the Divine Essence: Scriptum super libros Sententiarum, Book I Distinction 8* Binghamton University: Center for Medieval and Renaissance Studies, 1997.

Thomas Aquinas. *Summa Theologica*. Trans. by the Dominican Fathers of the English Province. New York, Benziger Bros., n. d.

Thompson, D'Arcy Wentworth. *On Growth and Form*. Cambridge University Press, 1917, revised 1942. New York: Dover reprint, 1992.

Urban, Wilbur Marshall. *Language and Reality: The Philosophy of Language and the Principles of Symbolism*. London: George Allen and Unwin, 1939.

Weiner, Bernard. "Reflections on the History of Attribution Theory and Research; People, Personalities, Publications, Problems." *Social Psychology* 39(3) (2008) 151–156.

Weizenbaum, Joseph. *Computer Power and Human Reason; From Judgment to Calculation*. San Francisco: W. H. Freeman, 1976.

Westphal, Merold. *God, Guilt, and Death; An Existential Phenomenology of Religion*. Bloomington: Indiana University Press, 1984.

Wilshire, Bruce. "Fifty Years of Academic Philosophy in the United States: Why the Failure of Nerve?" *Soundings* 67 (84/Winter) 411–419.

Wittgenstein, Ludwig. *Philosophical Investigations; The English Text of the Third Edition*. Trans. G. E. M. Anscombe. New York: Macmillan, 1958.

Zizioulas, John D. *Being as Communion: Studies in Personhood and the Church*. Crestwood, NY: St. Vladimir's Seminary Press, 1985.

Zizioulas, John D. *Communion and Otherness: Further Studies in Personhood and the Church*. Ed. Paul McPartlan. London: Continuum, 2006.

Index

Achnai, Oven of, 82
act
    definition, 62, 63, 77, 78, 100, 104
    human, 102–104
    of God, 39, 78, 95, 101–105
adaequatio intellectus et rei, 36
affirmation of human life in this world, 87, 108
Akiba, rabbi, 114
analogy, 99–102
    and ambiguity, 78, 79
    and univocation, 90
    Cajetan, 99
    divine action, 102
    human involvement, 37
    IV Lateran, 79, 101
    radial category, 37
analytic philosophy, 40, 93, 102
anamnesis, 114
anomie, 25
anthropology, 14, 28, 45, 48, 67, 68
anthropomorphic concept of God, 90, 102
Antigone, 11, 81
Aphrahat, 113
apophatic theology, 65, 66
approval, 102
Aquinas, 12, 24, 39, 76
    analogy, 99
    and Tillich, 97

Five Ways, 95, 97, 98
Super Sententiarum, 39, 60
transcendence, 98
truth, 36
Aristotle, 17, 23, 27
    action, 103, 104
    analogy, 99
    animal motion, 9
    ethics, 33
    existence of the world, 97
    formal cause, 76
    four causes, 111
    logic, 56
    Poetics, 103
    substance, 50
    truth, 36
Augustine of Hippo, 7, 46

Bale, Christian, 85
Ballard, James, 85
baptism, 89
basic life orientation, 69, 75, 76, 78, 79, 94, 108
behavior
    animal, 9, 11, 78
    human, 54, 113
being
    alone, 21
    composite, 76
    for us, 79
    in the world, 71

not-in-control, 79
toward persons, 41
with, 20–22
Berger, Peter, 7, 55, 75, 82
cosmogenesis, 25
Rumor of Angels, 69, 86
Social Construction, 23–30, 35, 91
Blair, Alexander, 48
Boethius, 51
Boole, George, 55
Brague, Rémi, 56
Buber, Martin, 14, 22, 45–49
Buddhism, 108
Bultmann, Rudolf, 4
Burrell, David, 95, 99

Cajetan (Tommaso de Vio), 99
cataphatic theology, 66
Catechism of the Catholic Church, 93
category error, 11, 38, 40, 96
deliberate, 40, 97, 102
Cauchy, Augustin-Louis, 38
Chalcedon, Definition of, 94
Chalcedonian method, 67
chaos, 24
Chomsky, Noam, 57
Church, Alonzo, 56
clearings, 18, 62, 69, 70, 79, 94, 104, 110, 113, 115
Coffey, David, 44
Common Documents, definition, 77
communion of persons, 13, 49–51
conceptuality, 77
contingency, *see* act
creationism, 40, 104

de Lubac, Henri, 44

despair, 6, 30–32, 59, 116
determinism, 76, 77
Laplacian, 76
Deuteronomic history, 92
Deuteronomist, 93
Dix, Gregory, 113
Dreyfus, Hubert, 8
coping, 61

Ellis, John M., 7, 8, 56–58, 79, 101
empiricism, 55
Euclid's Fifth Postulate, 2
evolution, 77, 78
existentiale, 23
Exodus
golden calf, 92
the Name, 100
typology, 77, 109, 111, 114

Feuerbach, Ludwig, 48
fideism, 98
Fides et Ratio, 68
Fingarette, Herbert, 10
formal cause, 3
Fraenkel, Abraham, 56
Franks, Curtis, 46
Frege, Gottlob, 55

Gödel, Kurt, 56
Gare St. Lazare, 9
Garrigou-Lagrange, 44
Genesis, 93
Golding, William, 85, 89

Hamilton, A. G., 38
Hegel, 30
Heidegger, 14, 45
and Aristotle, 17
authenticity, 24, 26, 32
being with, 20

Index

being-in-the-world, 15, 16, 19, 21, 36, 57–59, 61, 62, 77, 80
    Dasein, 15–21, 42, 45
    Daseinanalytik, 19, 29, 35
    definition of Dasein, 16, 23
    mistake on p. 12, 19, 20, 22, 29, 44, 45, 47, 73
Heidegger, Martin, 72
hermeneutical circle, 58, 63, 82, 90, 104
hermeneutics, 55, 76, 82
Higgs boson, 98
Hobbs, Edward, 77
    definition of theology, 61
    Limitation, 111
    suffering for others, 110
    the eighth interpretation, 77, 78
Hoyle, Fred, 19
Humean miracles, 40, 43, 67, 90, 104
hypostasis, 50
hypostatization, 66, 91, 92

idols, 92, 93
illusion, world as, 83
Incarnation, 109, 114, 115
Indo-European languages, 14
irony, 40, 61, 65, 75, 85–116
irrationalism, 98
Isaiah
    deutero-Isaiah, 105, 110
Israel struggles with God, 102

Jaspers, Karl, 69
Jeroboam son of Nebat, 92
Jesus, 77, 109–115
Job, 87, 89, 110

John of Damascus, 12, 40, 83, 95, 96
Judaism
    rabbinic, 109, 115
    Second Temple, 109

Kant, 97
    ethics, 33
    truth, 36
Kenny, Anthony, 72, 76
Kierkegaard, Søren, 13, 14, 30–32, 34, 42, 45, 46, 48
Kleene, Stephen, 56
Kuhn, Thomas, 58
Kyrie Eleison, 88, 89, 115–117

Lakoff, George, 37
language-capable life, 3, 6, 13, 18, 77, 81
languageability, 3, 18
Larson, Gary, 106
Latin language, 56, 87, 96
Lewis, C. S., 41–43, 55, 124
literalism, 90
logicism, 58
logos, 4
Luckmann, Thomas, 35, 75, 82, 86
    Social Construction, 23–30

Macintyre, Alasdair, 58
Marcionite crisis, 109
marine mammals, 77
Mascall, E. L., 51
materialism, 3, 18, 55, 76, 113
mattering, 6–8, 11, 15, 17–19, 22, 27, 36, 42, 54, 70, 76, 77, 79, 82, 83
    and composite bodies, 8, 77
    and criticism, 54

McClendon, James, 63
Mead, George Herbert, 33, 34, 43, 48
meaninglessness, 24, 25, 35, 58
mechanics
    quantum, 76
metanoia, 111
Michelangelo, 93
monophysite theology, 40
monotheism, historical, 93
Moses, 100, 114
Mulhall, Stephen, 40, 69, 102
Murray, John Courtney, 39, 100, 105
Myers, Doris T., 55, 58, 59

Nédoncelle, Maurice, 49
naiveté
    primary, 85
    secondary, 85
narrative coherence of a human life, 65, 78, 116
naturalism, 8, 76, 77, 82, 90, 103, 104, 113
Niebuhr, H. Richard, 14, 33–35, 60, 89, 101, 106
    Faith on Earth, 35
    Responsible Self, 33, 34
Niebuhr, Reinhold, 106
nihilism, 4, 56, 58, 59, 116
nominalism, 54, 55, 58, 76, 113
nominalization, 91
Nouvelle théologie, 44

O'Callaghan, John, 97
Oath Against Modernism, 95
objectivation, 25, 28, 43, 82, 83, 90–95, 97, 105
Oedipus, 10, 11

ontology
    and language, 26
    anxiety, 25
    distributed, 89, 100, 113, 116
    foils, 64, 111
    nanomind, 76
    of action, 61
    of humans, 19, 60, 70, 101
        and ambiguity, 106
        closed, 50
        interpersonation, 20–23, 25, 29, 33, 36, 41, 48, 49
        substance, 50
    of life, 6
    sociology, 23, 24, 28
    speech acts, 64, 113
    systems, 51, 91
    Work of Christ, 111, 114
ontotheology, 79
Oswald, Lee Harvey, 112

pan-psychism, 36, 91
Pascal, Blaise, 46
Passion, the, 109–114
Paul of Tarsus, 35, 110, 111, 113
Peirce, Charles Sanders, 56, 58
performative speech acts, 22
Pfeiffer, R. H., 110
Phillips, D. Z., 37, 38, 71, 98, 101
phlogiston, 61, 81
physics, 27
Pieper, Josef, 24
Placher, William, 66
Plato, 23
Platonism, 58, 60, 76, 79, 80, 116
    ideal forms, 54, 81
Playfair's axiom, 2
polytheism, 93
positivism, 10, 38, 39

power set, 77
prayer, 4, 10, 38–40, 86, 93
predicate calculus, 55, 58
presence-at-hand, 20, 21
proofs, 12, 13, 56, 65, 67, 90, 94–99, 107, 116
propositions, 10, 36, 37, 59, 61, 65–67, 89, 94, 99
providence, 102
Psalms, 86, 94
pseudo-Dionysius, 60, 83
purgatory, 116
Pyrrhonism, 59

Qoheleth, 110
Queneau, Raymond, 9, 10

Raff, Rudolf A., 9
Rahner, Karl, 13, 14, 44–45
rationalism, 90, 98
religion
    a social construction, 43
    biblical, 10, 12, 45, 64, 71, 78, 84, 87, 92, 102, 109, 110
    Christianity, 84, 109
    historical-covenantal, 92, 98, 111
    history of, 109, 115
    of nature, 92, 93
    philosophy of, 12, 37, 75, 93, 95, 97
    South Asian, 83
    world-affirming, 71, 111
repentance, 1, 2
responsible liberty of interpretation, 78, 82, 114
Resurrection, 82, 85, 90, 111
Ricoeur, Paul, 52, 62, 63, 85, 103
Rocca, Gregory, 39, 99

Rosser, J. Barkley, 56
Rubenstein, Richard L., 80
Rumpole, Horace, 81
Russell, Bertrand, 56

sacred canopy, 90, 114, 116
sardines, 26
Saussure, Ferdinand de, 56
Schleiermacher, Friedrich, 30, 67
scholastic philosophy, 17, 39, 44, 45, 99
science, 8, 24, 38, 51, 57, 61, 69, 76, 90, 91
Scotus, John Duns, 83
Second Jewish Revolt, 114
seers, 9
self
    self-being, 46–48
    self-relationship, 29–32
    selfhood, 29, 30, 32, 33, 61, 62, 64–65, 73
Septuagint, 35
Shakespeare, William, 64
shamans, 9
Sheehan, Thomas, 53, 72
    aletheia, 26, 36, 53
    clearings, 70
    Heidegger, 15, 16, 18–20, 22, 26, 27, 62, 70
    legein, 11, 15
    truth, 62
Shoah, 114
skepticism, 59, 60
socialization, 28
    and language, 55
    primary, 29, 80
    secondary, 28, 29, 80
sociology, 30, 34, 75, 84, 91, 115

of knowledge, 13–15, 23–30, 32, 35, 52, 58
solicitude, 47, 49
Sondheim, Stephen, 112
Sophocles
    Theban plays, 10
space aliens, 77
Spielberg, Steven, 85, 86
Steiner, George, 59, 60, 83
Stemberger, G., 2
Stoppard, Tom, 86
Strack, H. L., 2
substance, 48–50
success in life, 78
suffering, 10, 69, 110–114, *see* Hobbs
    Akiba, 114
    as foil, 107
    Jesus, 110, 114
    Rahner, 45
    Theban plays, 10, 11
    why this suffering?, 78, 110
supernatural
    existential, 13, 44–45
    modern, 67
system
    and mattering, 8
    Heidegger, 48
    ontology, 51

Talmud
    liberty of interpretation, 82
    Menahoth, 114
Ten Commandments, 93
Terrien, Samuel, 110
The Far Side, 106
Thompson, D'Arcy Wentworth, 9
Tillich, Paul, 97, 115
trajectories, 103

triumphalism, 60
truth
    adaequatio, 37
    aletheia, 18, 26, 27, 36, 53, 62, 70
    as correspondence, 36, 62
    troth, 37, 81, 82, 101, 107
Turing, Alan, 56

ultimate reality, 4, 48, 50, 54, 61, 78, 83, 87, 90, 94, 97, 98, 100, 102, 104, 105, 107–109, 113, 115, 116
unanswerable questions, 11, 39, 40, 56, 62, 67–70, 83, 89, 90, 96, 106, 108
uncanny, 61, 70
universals, 54
univocation, 90, 99, 100
Urban, Wilbur Marshall, 55

Vatican I, 95
via negativa, 60, 66
volokinesis, 104, 105
vorhanden, 17

Weidman, John, 112
Weierstrass, Karl, 38
Westphal, Merold, 83, 100
White Rose, the, 111, 112
Whitehead, Alfred North, 100
why, 37, 101
Williams, Charles, 14
Wittgenstein, Ludwig, 7, 18, 56, 76
    Tractatus, 53
Work of Christ, 109–114
Wright, Barbara, 10

Yahwist, 93

Zermelo, Ernst, 56
Zizioulas, John, 14, 49–51
zuhanden, 17

www.ingramcontent.com/pod-product-compliance
Lightning Source LLC
Chambersburg PA
CBHW050828160426
43192CB00010B/1944